Echt. 1970

THE WONDER OF WORDS

RICHARD CHURCH

The Wonder of Words

HUTCHINSON OF LONDON

HUTCHINSON & CO *(Publishers)* LTD
178-202 Great Portland Street, London W1

London Melbourne Sydney
Auckland Bombay Toronto
Johannesburg New York

First published 1970

*This book has been set in Bembo, printed in Great Britain
on Smooth Wove paper by Anchor Press, and
bound by Wm. Brendon, both of Tiptree, Essex*

ISBN 0 09 102230 4

★

To

D.M.C.

★

ACKNOWLEDGEMENTS

To Routledge & Kegan Paul Ltd. for quotation from
My Sad Pharaohs by Jack Bevan

To Faber & Faber Ltd. for quotation from *Collected Poems* by
T. S. Eliot and *Collected Poems* by Edmund Blunden

To Oxford University Press for quotation from *Experiences*
by Arnold Toynbee

To Methuen & Co. Ltd. for quotation from *Henry James at
Home* by Montgomery Hyde

To Rupert Hart-Davis for the quotation from *Prayer to the
Sun* by Phoebe Hesketh

# CONTENTS

Though I would not often assume the critic's privilege of being confident where certainty cannot be obtained

SAMUEL JOHNSON

PART ONE

Waking to words

1

The hand producing these words under the direction of the brain behind it has been practising in this medium of language for sixty years. Many millions of words, therefore, have been shaped and committed to paper by this team of five fingers and a presiding consciousness.

Maybe an ulterior power, the subconscious, has also played a part in the creative habit. But that is an assumption difficult to prove, though every professional writer recognises, and remembers, the unaccountable sensation of the words dropping from his pen during what are called 'inspired' moments.

There is a plaque on the wall of a house in the High Street of a village called the Bagni di Lucca in Tuscany which records that 'The English Poet, Shelley, when not possessed by the Divine Fire of composition, amused himself by dropping flowers over the balcony'.

So even municipal authorities, at least in Italy, also are aware of this irrational assumption that words can be produced by hand at the command of some power superior to the mind of the writer. But it is a dangerous assumption, more common to the novice and the dilettante than to the mature writer who has reached the middle, or is nearing the further, end of the desert in his quest for a few flowers.

Shelley's secondary hobby may have represented a desperate symbolism, the absent-mindedness of mental exhaustion after his failure to escape from the tyranny of certain words which persisted in repeating themselves throughout his writings, all of them betraying his preoccupation with transcendental ideas and moods: 'airy', 'inane', 'skyey', 'vast', 'clouds', 'ocean', and other words that are conjurations rather than statements, figures of cosmic significance rather than presentation of things observed.

Shelley, however, is instanced only as an extreme producer of words in this obsessed manner. All writers, in some degree, are similarly enslaved; even academics, technicians, lawyers and other persons whose committal of words to paper is utilitarian. Even those words refuse to lie down. They make a gesture, however feeble, that signifies the personality behind the hand that has produced them by means of a pen, a typewriter, a tape machine, or an amanuensis.

The strange thing is that the writer may not be strikingly idiosyncratic as a person in daily social life. He or she may be bumbling, stumbling, shy or a boring chatterbox, a smart business executive, or a naive recluse. Such characteristics, the surface feature, may disappear without trace as soon as that person puts pen to paper. Dr. Johnson said of Oliver Goldsmith that 'he wrote like an angel, and spoke like poor poll'.

There is much truth in the saying that you should never try to meet the author of a book which has moved you deeply. Often, the greater the book, the more impermeable the author. It is not always so, but it can be so. It is as though the 'virtue' which has been put into the writing leaves the author bereft; a widow's cruse.

That is my own experience, especially after a long session pen in hand. I emerge like a sleep-walker, even today after over half a century of learning to be economical in 'the expense of spirit' in a waste of words. By 'waste' I mean that verbal desert to which I have already referred. I do not mean that life itself is a desert. I am not like Leopardi, or James Thomson, the author of *The City of Dreadful Night*, who found it so. On the contrary, my trouble has been that life, the procession of phenomena, has always overwhelmed me by its dazzling speed, variety, beauty and forcefulness.

Added to that, the medium of language has piled Pelion upon Ossa by its vastness, complexity, mobile range and elusiveness. It persists in being a mirror to life, and is therefore equally intractable, dangerous, and prone to revelation which is more than that limited machine, the human brain, can absorb or digest.

Even the giants among us, Pythagoras, Dante, Leonardo,

Shakespeare, Newton, Goethe, experience that lifelong mental dyspepsia. What Goethe meant, crying out on his death-bed for 'More light! more light!', was that he despaired of the words. So did Shakespeare, in his last play, through the mouth of Prospero. 'We are such stuff as dreams are made of.' He too meant that the mirror was broken in his clumsy hands. And he was the greatest word-monger the human race has ever produced, so far as I know in my woefully limited knowledge of the mystery of language.

But these gigantic precedents need not make us despair, either in experiencing the ups and downs of life or in reflecting that experience by whatever instrument is most accommodating to our individual capability. The instrument which is primary and common to us all is language. A few of us raise that medium to make it an art. We are the writers, bold enough to claim (to hide our terror) that

> We are the music makers,
> We are the dreamers of dreams,
> We are the movers and shakers
> Of the world forever, it seems.

And the curious thing is that this is true, even today, in an explosive age in which man is exceeding all past achievement in developing the machinery of self-expression. Some contemporary prophets predict that the human race will soon be able to do without words by returning to a sort of inflated childhood, whose relation with the universe is purely visual, but on such a scale, microscopic and telescopic, as will reveal the final secret, or unfinal non-secret, of Creation. According to these forecasters (usually also broadcasters), languages will become comparable to Stone Age tools, the museum exhibits of linguistic archeologists and historians.

Already some academics in the universities, and in the magazines and newspapers that indulge in criticism of the arts, are contemptuous of aesthetic consideration about language. The grammar of form in speech and composition is dismissed as a relic of the sciolism of the Middle Ages, lingering through the paradox of revolt in the poetry and prose of the Romantic movement; words for words' sake. The magic phrase, the fulcrum of a balanced paragraph, the selection of a word whose *sound* conjures an atmosphere empathetically around its meaning; all these devices, familiar in the literatures of past civilisations, are being as ruthlessly questioned as are the metaphysics and dogmas of the religions of mankind.

The metaphor, the simile, the symbol, are thrown out of the aseptic laboratory into which the theorists (and indeed the activists) of the latter half of the twentieth century are dragging not only the human race but our mother earth and the empyrean in which we function. Function is the keyword; so much so, that I feel myself to be obsolete in using the word 'word'.

But this is merely a playful side-kick at a passing fashion. We have to appreciate the justifiable excitement and headstrong pride exhibited world-wide over the mechanical invention and fertility of our Machine Age. For the time being we have gone mad, like the Old Testament tribe which did so well in its colonisation that it began to worship the Golden Calf. We are worshipping the Computer, and all the other products of the engineer, the physicist, the chemist, disregarding the fact that they may provoke a monomania, lethal and destructive, as idolatry has done consistently throughout the millennia of our human story.

It is true that these modern instruments, so powerful that they already enable us to make excursions from our parent planet, and to tamper with the axioms of birth and death, are made with a diminishing use of the medium of language. The computer, the TV camera, the myriad gadgets used in every sophisticated activity of applied science, are wholly utilitarian and mechanical if it is necessary for them to include words in their functioning. And since we worship these latter-day creations of our own minds we tend to imitate them.

The orators, the poets, though as profuse and numerous as ever, have lost authority and influence. We see this by comparing the status of the art of letters today with that which it held only a century ago. And this is due not only to over-production of books and newsprint, not only to a democratic levelling-down of cultural and especially literary values. Our way of life itself, in every daily detail, is bypassing the library, the book, the printed word, in spite of the fact that each year is a record year in book production and newspaper circulation. Most of those books and newspaper articles, however, are a persistent dialogue on the desire to do away with words, to 'cut the cackle', as the mob on the factory floor, the sports arena, and in the 'palais de dance' hall would say.

Like all argument, however, such as I have lured myself into now, the prejudice produces counteraction; argument is a form of violence, and since it is verbal, solely weaponed with words, it contradicts in this present monologue all that I have said. It shows that through words a consciousness of the predicament of contemporary culture is still active. Words are still dominant, still in authority.

Thus returning full-circle, I have begun to ponder this medium of words, which I have been using for so many decades in a professional way. I am like an old gardener who has worked since his boyhood on his master's estate, and is now reluctantly preparing to retire. He is collecting his tools together; probably taking them with him to his cottage, half-doubtful of the intention to use them there on his tiny patch. He notices how the spade is shrunken, the tines of his fork shortened, the hoe reduced. But the wooden handles of all these tools of his craft are smoothed and polished by years of use. His hands have done that. It is their signature to the document of his life. I know that process in actuality, for like so many writers I have also made and maintained gardens. I inherited a spade from my father which time had perfected in weight, edge, familiarity. No new spade did the job so economically, cutting and turning the sod.

When the handle used by my father succumbed at last in my hands I had a new one fitted by the local blacksmith. That too became appropriate to my palms, smooth and polished. It is not long since I contemplated for the last time that accommodation between wood and flesh.

Now I look in the same way at a more subtle tool, 'my words to you, my words!' as Alice Meynell cried at the end of an impassioned love-poem. In this modern age to say that the usage of words with a creative purpose, especially in verse forms, is a declaration of love is likely to evoke derision. But it is true, for language begins by being an emotional impulse, an outcry of a birth-pang. Away back in the beginnings of the human race it was probably no more than a grunt. Through many drudging centuries it has evolved into the dialogues of Plato, the songs of Isaiah, and the vast chorus of man's vocal self-expression still recording the wonder, the joy, the agony with which he responds to the adventure of living. That chorus, the unceasing outpouring of words, is the challenge with which we all defy the eternal eliminator. We cry against it in our degree with Shakespeare:

> Yet, do thy worst, old Time: despite thy wrong,
> My love shall in my verse ever live young.

That love is the very breath we take, the rhythm of our blood, the mystery which still eludes the test-tube. We cannot deny it. Even the vitriol in which Voltaire and Jonathan Swift dipped their pens produced a variation of the love-letter.

2

That fanciful idea, which an austere critic will dismiss as a literary trope, brings me back to the original paradox that set me off on this enquiry, probably a useless one, as though a veteran painter should stop work with his brushes to peer at the confusion of colours smeared over the palette balanced on his arm. Did Turner have that experience, prior to the outburst of colour delirium which produced his later pictures? If it might have an equivalent effect on my future writings I should not worry. Behind the frenzy of those wild water-colours and those vast canvases can still be traced the structural craftsmanship, the architecture, the economy of suggested form.

I suspect that those later products of Turner's art are only an exaggeration of the process by which every artist matures. It is desirable, if he is to endure through full and venerable growth, that he should start under discipline, apprenticed to the technique, mastering its formality, rooting himself firmly in its tradition, so that when the winds of fashion rage he shall not be toppled over into eccentricity and even fraudulent tricks.

Experience brings habitual command of technique, and a move towards that ease and economy which cover up all signs of effort, and transmute the technique, the craftsmanship, into second nature, the partner of intuition. So in their late work poets, composers, painters, all artists, tend towards simplicity; but a simplicity which is enigmatic, oracular, subtle. The medium becomes like a spider's web in its seeming fragility, almost sinister in its ability to capture truth, that otherwise elusive fritillery.

So here I find myself halted; a frightening pause, as of a cessation of footsteps heard in an otherwise silent and foggy night. So too the sound of my words has stopped; the myriads of them that have been tramping through my life, sometimes dreadful and ominous, sometimes with drum and fife, a vast

B

army carrying me along, rather as an urchin or camp-follower than a trained soldier.

For what instantly daunts me in this critical pause, this silence which is a momentary penumbra round the brink of total voicelessness into which we all must relapse, is that I know nothing about the words which I have dared to call my medium, my profession, over sixty years. Even the fact that writers leave a record of their activity after they have fallen upon eternal silence does not reassure me. We have, in old age, no certainty of our technical command. We ask ourselves if, after all, long practice and experience do bring the authoritative touch? Did not young Chatterton, young Keats, achieve that? Was not the infant Mozart born to a command of his medium, absolute and mature? It is hardly an exaggeration to agree that this was so. Then what have the veteran practitioners to offer as a claim to authority? I have already likened their skill to that of the spider. It has a touch of horror, and may explain much about the eternal revolt of youth against age, 'crabbed age', as Shakespeare subtly called it. Is this what students all round the world are revolting against, the webs spun by the old, in politics, morals, dogmas, art forms?

But it is inevitable that work, continued through years against adversity, indifference, the languors of body and brain, the temptations of our emotions and all the waywardness of passion, should have to be bolstered up by discipline. A substantial building, even a modern one, still needs scaffolding while being erected.

The scaffolding round the house of language, however, has become a specialist's concern, like that of the workmen who precede the bricklayers and masons. In the structures of words we have our academics, our grammarians. If they become too assiduous their eternal skeletal erections restrict the architect of words, the poet, or indeed any user of language striving to be vividly expressive.

That happens in all academics, since it creates a dogma. It

leads to hierarchy, as in religion, and in the end the priests crucify the Christ.

Youth has always rebelled against that hardening process. The young cannot see that this is a natural process, the tree enclosing itself in bark, massing its roots obstinately in the soil in order to sustain the ever-increasing speed and weight of foliage against the storm of time. Growth without hardening was an experiment which nature abandoned as a failure in the Squashy Periods, myriads of centuries ago.

Every artist, whatever medium he chooses or is chosen by, has to become aware of that failure in the experiment by evolution of the flora and fauna of the earth to which he is committed both as instrument and instrumentalist. At times when human society, like the growing serpent, is shedding a skin the younger generation ignores this natural example. That is happening in the twentieth century, with temporarily squalid developments. The giant, shapeless slug has reappeared.

During such a period of social turmoil, with world-wide new orientations taking shape, all manner of experimental chicane is permitted, each contradicting the other, in religious beliefs, in politics and administration, and in the arts. Ancient superstitions, fashionably disguised, are acclaimed by the bewildered young as novelties. They make a noisy traffic wearisome and familiar to older ears.

But when was there not social turmoil; when was there not this conflict of ideologies protesting against the stablility coagulated from the upheavals of preceding generations? History, if studied in depth and detail, shows no periods of complete acceptances. The Roman Catholic Church, which was believed to have imposed an authoritative unity during the Middle Ages, did no such thing. Its internal dissensions began immediately the apostles were left alone to plan the opening stages of their evangelism, armed only with a bewildering myth and the Gift of Tongues. The quarrels and arguments are recorded in the *post-obit* chapters of the New Testament, coloured by the characters and abilities of the writers of the Epistles, Paul, Peter, James, Luke, Barnabas, Silas, Apollos, Priscilla. We cannot assuredly sort them out. Nothing is certain about this astounding claim which even today dominates all theories in the Western world by which human society might be stabilised in peace.

But there was a consistency of vision in one of that group endowed miraculously with this Gift of Tongues. We still use the phrase, though in our age of rationalism, and need for scientific verification, we can accept it only as a metaphor. That consistent man was the apostle John, 'whom Jesus loved'.

His consistency was in his single-minded reiteration of the idea of the authority of words. It expresses itself in the first sentence of his gospel, in which he stated that 'God is the Word' and has been so from the Beginning. What does it mean? A vast literature of commentary surrounds it, accumulated by theologians and philosophers over nearly two thousand years. But today we do not even know what theology is, other than a study of folklore, mythology, psychological symbolism.

The ancient universities of Europe are still heavily endowed with Chairs of Theology. What do their professors produce today; what elucidations do they make, as the chemists, physicists, astronomers, mathematicians, engineers, doctors and alienists, explore and explore and explore, into the depths of time and space, the sources and functioning of the universe and the human mind that observes it, and is conditioned by it?

There is no convincing answer. But out of the bewilderment, the contradictions and scepticism, there still rings the voice of this one man John (though his identity tends to become apocryphal) claiming that 'The Word' was in the Beginning, and was God.

Again I ask, what does it mean? It is so persistent. At the end of the New Testament it rings out afresh like an angelus bell over the ruined landscape of a battlefield, whence the 'captains and kings' have departed, and the blood has soaked into the soil poisoned by cruelty. This man John, the poet amongst the executives and administrators who took charge of the newly born Christian Church and made it into an Institution, cries out again in his Book of Revelations (comparable to the ravings of Swedenborg and William Blake). He sees the aftermath of that battle.

> Then I saw the dead, great and small, standing before the throne *and the books were opened*. And the dead were judged by *what was written in the books*.

So this strange visionary, this poet who figures in Leonardo's picture of the *Last Supper* resting with his head on the bosom of Christ, begins his evidence, and ends it, in terms of *The Word*. What is that Word? What are those Books? How do we interpret this symbolism, if we can accept it as no more than that?

But symbolism, and the whole fabric of mythology which is woven from it, is known today to have an authenticity as assured as that of scientific knowledge. Indeed we analyse facts and find them to be composed of symbols, representing further, deeper, subtler facts, which again refer symbolically to more remote subdivisions of the material of the universe, or more probably the universes, which 'were in the Beginning', which were *The Word*.

This was the man who foretold 'a new heaven and a new earth'. It is all quite incomprehensible. But it has a validity because it presents the instrument by which human nature has discovered within itself the faculty of awareness, of consciousness, which must have been 'in the Beginning'. It presents the power and authority of language; 'the Word'. So this mystical figure, this visionary whose symbols, mythological references, apocalyptic, terrifying and supreme in their promise of a creative outcome to human history 'after the sea gives up its dead', begins his testimony, not only with a symbol, but with a scientific fact. Language is *actually* the instrument. The Word is *really* the tool by which man has become man, capable of crying out, as no other natural creature can cry out 'Death, *thou* shalt die!'

3

The art of the writer begins from there. But what is that 'art', what is its craft, and how long does the apprenticeship last? Moden techniques of teaching literacy, like those of teaching a foreign language, have speeded up the process, mainly by aural and oral methods. With the instruments of radio, and recording machines, elementary instruction in the use of language has gone back to the forum and the methods of ancient Mediterranean cultures. This may lead to a resurrection of rhetoric, latterly suspect, as a means of communication, thus restoring to social gesture and political debate a ceremonial element that will slow down the speed with which contemporary life surges on with no deterrent towards catastrophe. Language used as an art is a brake as well as an incitement. We pause to listen, and more frequently desist from doing the wrong thing than the wise thing.

I have noticed, in children taught the conscious use of their native language by those modern methods, that the result is a coolness of mood, an ease of self-expression, a *civilised* attitude, which came belatedly, if at all, to children at elementary or kindergarten schools at the beginning of the twentieth century, when compulsory education was only some thirty years in action. I asked a grandson recently if he did not feel the cold of an English winter severely. He is twelve years old, and has spent the past seven of them in tropical countries. He replied that he did not, for 'fortunately I am rather stout'. The wording of that phrase has an echo of formal speech such as Dr. Johnson or Gibbon used in the eighteenth century, Dickens or Gladstone in the nineteenth. This boy is not an addicted reader, nor is he a school swot. He has learned by these modern methods which have, no doubt, given him direction in contact with parental conversation.

My own infantile experience was different from that, nearly

seventy years earlier. My environment was working class and lower-middle class, two 'castes' which at the end of the Victorian age lived interwoven but without mixing, even though their children sat together from the age of five years in the elementary schools in London.

I remember vividly the first impressions of being taught the alphabet, then words of two or three letters, and so progressively to simple sentences, and the elements of syntax and parsing. Thus began the introduction to the science of grammar, which was carried on from the infant school to the upper school, where a parallel process began in the French language.

But the significant thing which I want to distinguish is that all this was done with the help of the blackboard, and primary grammar books. It meant visually memorising, thus learning to spell, a skill which in English is wildly irregular, and lacking consonance with the spoken word.

It is worth noting, by an disdainfully modern educationist, that this curriculum was customary in a primary or what was called a board school, where other subjects, arithmetic, elementary geometry (known as 'Euclid'), geography, history, art and carpentry, were also part of the syllabus. We started school at 8.50 a.m., broke at 12 for midday meal (at home, not at school), reassembled at 1.50 and worked on until 5 p.m. Then we had 'homework'.

That discipline was, I think, a deterioration into laxity from the regime imposed by John Wesley in the school which he ran in the eighteenth century. His pupils, as Southey records in the biography of this man who forestalled the excesses of the French Revolution from setting fire to the English social structure, began their day's schooling at 5 a.m. and continued with short intermissions for meals and play until 9 p.m.

My own reaction to Victorian schooling was at first an utter bewilderment. For two years I stared at that blackboard and saw only a whitish blur against the dusty, sombre background. Nor could I make anything of those misty hieroglyphs. 'Dog and

cat' may have 'sat on the mat', but I could not learn to commu-
nicate that intelligence. All too frequently the frustration was
aided by a curtain of tears, the chagrin due to the teacher's rebuke
or sarcasm at my mental deficiency.

One day a medical officer inspected the infants, and I remember
standing between his knees while he looked solemnly at me
and told me to tell my parents that unless I was fitted with
spectacles I should be blind by the time I was fifteen. As I was
only seven at that time, I was not alarmed by so distant a fate.
The outcome of this threat, however, was that I was taken to the
local optician, where a miracle was worked which completely
altered my universe; I have described this in some detail in a
book called *Over the Bridge*, and I need not repeat that attempt
to capture the revelation.

From that day, when I looked at the blackboard in the classroom of sixty huddled and odorous infants, the 'cat' really did
'sit on the mat', emphatically and spellably. What is more, one
Saturday I took up a book borrowed by my brother (four years
my senior) from the public library; I sat down with it at the
kitchen table, opened that book at the first page, and *began to
read*.

I was not at the time conscious of this second miracle. I was
too much occupied with the abundance of the island, and the
persons of *The Swiss Family Robinson* so conveniently wrecked
on it. I still remember the names of the sons, Fritz, Ernest and
little Franz, and I can still see the palm trees overshadowing
the strand.

Only when I had finished reading my first book did I realise
that something unaccountable had happened. From being unable
to put two letters of the alphabet together to make a word of one
syllable, a process which formerly stunned me into imbecility,
my eyes could now transmit compounded words, sentences,
paragraphs, as smoothly as my throat could swallow a glass of
milk.

I tried out this intoxicating faculty on my father's newspaper, called the *Daily Chronicle*, and was transported to South Africa, where the British Army was in a most humiliating situation. Reading was no longer a schoolroom bewilderment; it was a natural function, like eating and drinking. I did not know then that the poet Coleridge had captured that experience in his phrase 'For he on honeydew hath fed, and drunk the milk of Paradise'.

That is how it was and how it has remained for the following seventy years. I still cannot explain the abruptness of that leap into literacy. Could a pair of spectacles, correcting myopia inherited from my mother, have been the sole instrument? If so, they were as authoritative as the sword of the Angel Gabriel.

That was the beginning of this preoccupation which has filled my life and directed my occupation. Unfortunately, I was not equipped with an intellectual vigour which might have taken up instantly this sudden endowment. I was a sickly child, and therefore too much sheltered and lazy. Long spells away from school let me escape the mental discipline and combative circumstances necessary to pronounce a personality and exercise a brain in acquiring knowledge and the obstinacy of staying-power. My mother was a school-teacher in another board school, even more 'ragged trouser' than the one I attended. My father was a minor civil servant, concerned only that my brother and I should follow him into a career that ensured security and a pension. It was a pardonable neurosis in those days before the creation of the Welfare State. Conditions then were the same as those at the beginning of the nineteenth century. I might, like the young Dickens, have been condemned to the Blacking Factory.

But the way of life in those lower-middle-class homes, encapsulated in social fears, caste-ridden both downward and upward, cannot be used as an excuse for intellectual timidity and idleness. The elements of French were taught at the board school, and I fastened on to that, but somewhat tentatively and without the burning fury with which I continued to consume and digest my native language, gulping down its poly-syllables with zest, a verbal glutton.

There was one inadequate dictionary in the little suburban home, and I appropriated it, carried it up to my bedroom and hoarded it there, like a miser with a bag of gold coins.

I had no direction from school to get hold of Latin and Greek dictionaries and primers. Thus I have gone through life with an unnecessary inferiority complex in this matter of verabl proficiency and command. I still, as a veteran in the profession of word-mongering, look with envy and a sense of guilt at people educated at grammar schools, public schools and universities. A man from Balliol, or King's College, Cambridge, makes me shiver with nakedness. Even the subsequent and not infrequent experience of speaking at some such schools and both these universities, and discovering the equivalent deficiencies amongst their students and staffs, has not cured me of the conviction of my intellectual and scholastic poverty. I still compare myself with so many Scottish dominies, sons of mountain shepherds, who by sheer will-power and northern mental vigour mastered the Hebrew of the Old Testament and the archaic Greek of the Iliad. James Hogg, the 'Ettrick Shepherd', taught himself to write by persevering on a patch of sand with his crook, while minding his flock. I wonder if so concentrated a purpose had an hypnotic effect, and passed some of this solitary scholarship to his dog?

The famous professor at Oxford, W. P. Kerr, linguistic savant and literary critic, master of many languages living and dead, began in the same way and in the same remote countryside.

I recall such careers with shame and humility, like the servant who buried his one talent, afraid or too idle to exploit it. The curious thing is that I can think of no better endowment than the gift of tongues. Whenever I read of that moment in the upper room when this amazing armoury was given to the apostles, prior to their dispersal over the Mediterranean world to preach the new gospel of compassion and the sanctity of the individual, I feel my blood glow in my cheeks. That 'if only' machinery of conscience, possessed in some degree by even the least intelligent mortal, is set in motion.

But we have to work with the various combinations that make up our characters; circumstances, which include environment, chance and luck, degrees of will-power, physical and intellectual equipment. We cannot all be like Goethe, with everything in his favour; wealth, social and political advantage, a powerful intellect and an artist's imagination, a native language still awaiting literary fulfilment and maturity.

We are all influenced, whatever our field of achievement, by the period into which we are born. John Addington Symonds, writing the history of the arts in Renaissance Italy, clarified this theory, a byway of Darwinism which later the pessimistic German Spengler carried further, to show that civilisations, human cultures, have an organic cycle of life.

Elderly folk usually accept Spengler's conclusion that the Western European civilisation is in its late autumnal period, especially in its linguistic aspects. Our languages, with their literatures, are overfull, overripe, dropping from the tree. That is the argument of people sophisticated by age. Many critics accept it, and if they are of a younger generation they propose either to prune the tree and graft a new aesthetic on it, or to uproot it altogether and burn it along with its label 'Tradition'.

This process is vast, universal. It affects every human activity and interest. In language and literature, which still survive as the probable currency of any future civilisation, we see how worn the coinage has become. The defacement of linguistic values did not begin lately, though the spread of semi-literacy has speeded up the process. Printed matter for the masses of humanity has rubbed away the poetic precision of words. They are no longer a golden coinage.

Compare two literary products using the same theme, the legend of King Arthur, the knights of the Round Table, and the adultery of Queen Guinevere and Lancelot. The prose version was written in the fifteenth century by a Lancastrian partisan politician named Mallory. It was one of Caxton's early imprints, in 1484. Though the form is prose, and the narrative loosely constructed, the *language*, the words, still gleam like medieval jewellery. The English tongue was then in its youth, and it fitted to the romantic theme like a glove to a girl's hand, as an artifice that was at the same time natural, unselfconsciously acceptable. Even this author, a worldling, not particularly specialist in letters, could not go wrong with this gracious, newly tempered tool. He was fortunate in his historical, cultural period.

When Tennyson, four hundred years later, put the same theme, taken from Mallory, into verse form, the change in the cutting edge of the tool was apparent, even when handled by a master musician in words. Those words, though mellifluous, had lost their lustre. The language had become tired with an equivalent of metal fatigue. Tennyson was unfortunate in his period.

So are we all today.

4

That is not an admission of pessimism or despair. The cycles of history, like the weather, have their seasons, beyond the control of individual men and women. Our human story is one of achievement with or against the favour of those odds; they supply a kind of counterpoint to our mortal melody, and we have to state that melody so that it shall run unbroken over this *basso ostinato* which swells or subsides below it.

Since 1914 the drums have dominated. They have gone berserk and savage as Africa plays so loud a part in the history of the twentieth century. Those drums are summoning the warriors out of the forests and the jungle. The din drowns the music of our Western culture. Our younger generations are hypnotised by it. In various disguises those drums have insinuated their threatening rhythms into all our arts, using our new mechanical devices as allies; suborning our electronics, our engineering symbols. I see, for example, the genius shown by Picasso in his early work, the superb drawing and sense of design, perverted by this African savagery. But that metamorphosis is popular. It has been imitated everywhere. The equivalent influence in music is equally remarkable. So, too, our use of language; our use and abuse of our native European tongues. The African drum-beat, out of the steaming jungle, is summoning mankind to bloodlust war, to nihilism, to destruction of all that has contributed over three millennia towards the structure of European civilisation. The relentless throbbing rises and falls, and draws ever nearer, ever more insistent, and frighteningly armed with our latest machinery of mechanics and philosophic probings and permissive moral and social values.

This is a statement of fact, not of ideology. The Western world at present is going that way, every change speeded up and magnified by the dreadful instruments of publicity, the pressures of closer and closer communication.

Does this mean that this Western way of life is coming to an end? But what of that? Has it been so virtuous, so serene, that it should be made sacred? There are a thousand answers, from the politicians, the sociologists, the theologians, the historians, the aestheticians, contending as groups and also contradicting each other within their own preserves.

Nor are the theorists of language at one. Purists repine over the discarding of classical schemes of grammar, vocabulary and syntax. Other scholars welcome the looser constructions, the neologisms, the tendency towards a sort of basic *lingua franca* suitable to the violent, supersonic speed with which the whole human race is intermingling.

The change is most obviously to be noted in journalism. Compare a leader written twenty years ago in *The Times*, or even in one of the larger circulation newspapers, with one in this morning's columns. The pace is different. The vocabulary is cut down today, to give speed of communication. Neologisms and slang abound. The prose is 'with it' to suit the immediacy of the theme, and also the unconscious assumption that the pressure of interests demands speed and superficial reference.

But this influence of verbal economy, sophisticated in its up-to-date imagery, is in conflict with the processes of modern methods of teaching literacy, which I have already described. Thus a mild schizophrenia possesses our young people. They are trying to travel simultaneously at two different speeds. The attempt creates a kind of mental drag, an intellectual giddiness, that affects the emotional balance. Our young folk can neither linger and savour, nor hurry on in order to miss nothing. Maybe this confusion adds to the sense of being cheated, that social malaise which is causing the violent unrest amongst students throughout the world. It may be the cause of that unrest having so indefinite à programme.

I listen to their spokesmen, the voices singled out by chance on television, or by newspaper interviewers, and the articulation, the vocabulary, the frenetic interpolation of the 'you know', the sign of verbal inadequacy, and I recognise the symptoms of a sick language, a language losing its gesture, its range and authority, its self-supporting expressiveness. Precision of speech, the full, round production of vowels, and the complete enunciation of consonants, which used to be the verbal habit of a rightly educated and civilised person, is now regarded as an affectation, an affront to the equalitarian vernacular through surly elision, the lowest common verbal denominator by which modern society communicates. Even professional speakers, actors, preachers, politicians, adopt this mangled, adenoidal delivery, deliberately prostituting pronunciation for fear of being accused of class distinction and superiority.

But to follow this argument into political and cultural analysis is outside my purpose. It would also cause accusations of my being reactionary and snobbish, because today is an era of revolution, and as always under such conditions, as history records, the violence of events and the putting of ideologies into practice lead always to confusing the good with the bad. The guillotine is still with us, indiscriminately at work, decapitating our vowels and consonants as well as the tyrannies of a society whose values are still based on money and primitive material gratification.

I am doubtful, however, if it is possible to dismiss from this book the horrible reality into which the actualities of speech have been dragged in our British community. Much of the rancour and resentment felt by the majority of folk towards good and musical speech are due to confusing it with the verbal affectations adopted by both intellectual and social snobs. But those affectations are as debased as the metropolitan, pinched nasal argot of the slums. All are weeds in the wheat of nourishing intercommunication on which a healthy society should feed. Clear pronunciation induces clear thinking, and controls passion. Gabbling, slurring, whining, muttering, set up mental and emotional fog, which causes the head-on crashes between individuals, or groups, within a community supposed to be native in the same language. The international misunderstandings that lead to perpetual suspicion and wars are not only due to economic and racial differences. They have persisted since the building of the Tower of Babel. One reason why the Christian Faith almost achieved a temporary cohesion of Western European society in the Middle Ages was that its administrative and executive officers had a concise common language—Latin. Even with that artifice, human nature could not bring its unique suicidal savagery under control. Maybe mathematics, deified today through the idols of the Computer and the Hydrogen Bomb, may make mankind coherent in benevolence and mutual constructiveness. Under these gods we are grasping at the moon. Maybe at last they will make us get down to earth.

5

Meanwhile, I am trying to get down to this common, everyday matter of speech: the words we use, why and how we use them, and what is the result. Simple things, fundamental things, are always complicated, always elusive. Here is a perpetual paradox. If, as scientists or philosophers, with highly sophisticated techniques, we probe into those simplicities, we find ourselves in the labyrinth.

For centuries they have been called 'elements', either of this world, as air, fire, water, earth, or of the shadow world of the mind towards which we grope; as love, worship, and the other intangibles that hover above the material universe, like the overtone of bell-music, commanding it to harmony.

But for the poet the 'word' is what the 'atom' is for the physicist, seemingly ever divisible, ever escaping into some 'backward and abysm of time' and space.

Plodding along the roads of philology and semantics, the grammarian, that scientist of language, does valuable work in tracing the origins and relationships of the multitude of tongues still confused so loudly and dangerously to a mischief symbolised in that poetic image of the Old Testament Tower of Babel. He brings fuel to the poet's fire, but he does not kindle it. Indeed, the history of human cultures suggests that the poet has preceded the grammarian, conjuring out of the social subconscious those verbal shapes on which the grammarian subsequently works, as recorder and custodian.

At seminal periods in the evolution of a language an individual poet has sown the seed and produced the first crop, to nourish a community and provide it with a standard of patent and recognisable communication. Homer and Hesiod, Livius Andronicus, Firdousi, Dante, Chaucer, Villon, Goethe, Pushkin, are such people, who at the right moment in the evolution of a language have gathered it together and folded its myth and

c

vernacular within a corpus of literary art to give it an aesthetic authority, both in the market place and in the library, on which the man in the street and possibly greater writers may draw.

But even this historical reference does not bring us to the heart of the mystery, the secret of that living force in the word. By that living force I mean the power which language exercises everywhere, and on all occasions, public and private, emotional and intellectual. Even to refer to this power is to labour the obvious. The dullest individual, hardly more than imbecile, takes this power of language for granted, and reacts to it even in the solitude of his own consciousness through thoughts framed in unspoken words. The lunatic, so far as one can observe him, stimulates himself to his frenzy, his delusions through a soliloquy of words, unspoken maybe, but nevertheless shaped in his diseased mind and thus the motive of his actions.

Public words, the war-cries of primitive savages, the reiterated slogans mouthed by mobs drunk on ideologies or the social phenomenon of mass hysteria, have the demonic power of feeding the excitement by which they are engendered. When we watch the television screen (and thus temporarily become indifferent gods above the battle of life) and see processions of crowds with banners surging along on a tidal wave of passion and protest we notice faces here and there, close-up for a second, then sucked back into the mêlée; we see an open mouth, chanting or screaming, 'Shakespeare *out*! Beauty *out*! Truth *out*!' or some such inflammation.

That inflammation is stoked by the word, the strange fuel, the same fuel that Iago used, with subtler and more penetrating art, to poison Othello's mind

> Look, where he comes! Not poppy, nor mandragora,
> Not all the drowsy syrups of the world,
> Shall ever medicine thee to that sweet sleep
> Which thou ow'dst yesterday.

Yet if we accept that words murdered Desdemona and

destroyed Othello we are merely taking the husk and ignoring the germ, the seminal power which makes language continuous and perpetually influential in human affairs, pioneering all experiment and evolution, and, alas, all destruction.

It is this vital content within the word that is the writer's responsibility. It is his raw material, more obdurate than the stone that challenges the sculptor or the mathematical scales that ultimately confine the musician no matter how mechanically he may try to transcend them.

The writer's raw material, language, is more difficult to master because it is also used in everyday life, as the universal utilitarian medium of communication, of joining individual to individual, of cementing society, of recording its transactions in time and space and of regulating their recurrence.

Thus the material in which the writer works is already man-handled, rubbed and soiled by superstition, habit, fashion, pre-conception. There are no Carrera quarries to which he can retreat, fastidiously to select an unsullied mass of marble for his purpose. Words are not so static. They have not been waiting, like Keats's Titan, 'Silent as a stone', virginal for the artist's touch.

Nor are they wholly aerial, like the sounds which the musician may conjure out of the pure mathematics flowing through the staves, by 'touching the tender stops of various quills'.

Words are common stuff; degraded in the gutters of civilisation, stale from constant exposure, misshapen and distorted by brutal and careless use. The writer, if he is to make anything memorable or authoritative out of them, has to restore their original virtue, repair their significance, reset them in the framework of a phraseology newly designed to make them attract and then compel the attention of peoples so burdened with language that its usage is comparable to wading through shingle: so many words, endless myriads of words, rounded by the tides of time into a pebbled uniformity.

6

This is the medium that I chose, or was chosen by, in boyhood, at that time between infancy and adolescence when all manner of unexpected experiences disturb the close, animal comfort of childhood, that state hardly less confined and protected than in the ante-room of life, the mother's womb.

It is a time of tremendous drama, based on the first awareness of being alone. The umbilical cord is cut at our birth, but there is another severance which has to be made before we are launched upon the ocean of consciousness. It comes with puberty, and it is a major release. The newborn child screams physically in order to take its first breath. At the second severance, as we are expelled from childhood, our minds scream inwardly. Desperate excitement, bewildering and enchanting as well as terrifying, stirs us into wakefulness; our horizons rush away in wild centrifugality, and we realise that we have to fend for ourselves, spiritually and mentally, in spite of the pilot guidance of parents, elders, school life, university or wherever we may spend those apprentice years.

Some people never cut that second cord. They stay anchored in the maternal harbour, unaware because they may disguise it as some adult subterfuge: a cosy marriage, a cloistral academic life, a religious dogma—any form that gives the illusion of safety. They never learn, or learn too late at the end of a cringing life, that there is no safety between birth and death. 'For we are born in others' pain, and perish in our own.'

One of the dangers of the Welfare State is that it encourages this basic timidity. The bureaucratic benevolence is necessary, as a social medicine, against the diseases of industrialism, but by giving people an expectation of security it blindfolds them against reality, and they do not see that this natural world is still the jungle, of which their own human nature is partly a composition.

But the rebuttal of this criticism is that civilisation itself works towards the same end, to master man's environment as well as the savage within him. Where it succeeds does it not so disturb the balance that its children become effete? Nineveh, Babylon and ancient Rome; where are they?

Something of that Rome survives in its literature, its words. As its most marmoreal poet said, '*si fractus illabatur orbis, imparvidum ferient ruine*'. 'When this world is shattered, I shall be riding on the pieces.'

That is characteristic of the vainglory common in the profession of letters: an occupational disease. But there is some justification for the statement, and we should note that it was made by a classicist, a sane and formal courtier contentedly housed on the bounty of Maecenas, his millionaire patron. He was thus no headstrong Romantic, like Shelley, who waved his apologia for poetry like a banner against the increasingly dominant philistinism of Western Europe at the beginning of the nineteenth century, when what William Blake called 'the dark, Satanic Mills' made such a triumphant din that the voice of humanity was drowned, even though Keats could still hear the nightingale in Hampstead.

Shelley asserted that 'poets are the unacknowledged legislators of the world', while Wordsworth, older and more deeply convinced, claimed that 'poetry is the light that is in the face of all science'.

If today, however, we writers do not believe that these extravagances are true, then we are doomed to defeat. Society will repudiate and ignore us. It has already begun to do so. No young poet writing today would dare to pontificate so loudly for his profession. He would at once be reduced to the ranks; for contemporary poets tend to march in cohorts, auxiliaries in the various armies conscripted for the intellectual armageddon of the twentieth century. The individual literary talent, and even the genius, wears the uniform of one or other ideology, raging in this world-wide un-free for all; and in the name of Freedom!

Amid all this, a writer of the generation born in the seemingly static Vicoria era is at a loss. He feels as though, present at a violent eruption of Etna, with disaster and destruction around him, he is pausing to polish his spectacles and readjust his hearing-aid. But he has a good precedent in those words of Horace two thousand years ago.

Thus I maintain my irrelevance, believing that all those past claimants of the authority of the Word are perpetually being justified by its survival over events. With Thomas Hardy's 'man harrowing clods', and his 'maid and her wight', who go about their business in the time 'of the breaking of nations', so the poet, the wielder of words, shall be concerned with that practice, knowing that

> War's annals will cloud into night
> Ere their story die.

It is no simple matter, however, to look back over one's lifetime concern with words, to discover what is 'their story' and how in one's own consciousness, in one's mind, in one's bones, it began.

7

It began for me only a few years after the first stage in the
development of literacy, when at the age of seven I suddenly
began to read. That was a complete metamorphosis, something
which happened seemingly, within an hour, like a butterfly
emerging from the chrysalis. No doubt the pupa within that
obdurate case had been evolving through a slow awareness of
those words of one syllable chalked on the blackboard in the
schoolroom, but the moment of change remains inexplicable.

In a moment, at the touch of an invisible wand, my eyes and
intelligence absorbed sentences, paragraphs, even the multi-
syllabic jargon of leading articles in the stately newspapers of
1900.

I may have been a slow starter, belated in my initiation. Sir
Compton Mackenzie, one of the most versatile and prolific
wielders of language in the twentieth century, states in his
autobiography that this mysterious experience of acquiring
literacy happened to him at the age of two. I do not doubt it,
for what happened to me was just as mysterious. I sprang from
absolute verbal darkness into light, instantly after the correction
of myopia by a pair of spectacles. Had the visual mechanical
defect of misshapen eye-balls held me back? Was the delay an
equally mechanical malformation in my infant brain cells? Or
was the revelation what we call 'an act of God', the useful
general term for most of the primary eventualities in the universe?
That term is anathema to the psychologists, but it still has a
packaging value. It protects us during the rough weather of
dire circumstances; sometimes even from the volcanic eruptions
and mind-quakes within each individual consciousness.

From the age of seven I used words in a matter-of-fact way,
as do most people. They conveyed only information. I treated
words with no more interest than the smoker treats the package
containing the cigarettes for which he craves. I wanted to live

more fully than a child was capable of living in those late Victorian days in suburban London. I did it by reading. I wanted a story. I wanted a definition of things, places, dramatic events. The words had to make something exist, something happen.

Professional writers, concerned with technique, tend to forget that what most people want from a book is exactly what I wanted during that interim stage of my lifelong love-affair with words. The words have to be transparent. They must not obscure the content.

It is a healthy demand. It is indicative of the springtime of life, both individual and racial. It brushes aside that sign of autumnal decay, 'art for art's sake', the late leaf, slightly etiolated, the word too many and too late.

This utilitarian usage of words survives through the ages as the norm. Language functioned thus in the first scripts, the clay tablets of Chaldea, Egypt, Crete. Most of the transcripts show those tablets to be bills of lading, or other statistical records. The words did not really matter, once they had done their job of conveyance.

So it is still, even in an over-sophisticated inter-racial society. Words are used mainly to inform, instruct, command, request. They are put to an even more elementary purpose on occasions of riot, or public demonstration, when the slogan is abbreviated in sense and magnified in sound, to become no more than an animal howling, as of the voices of the jackal and the wolf. Those noises are still words, but in a degraded denomination. Man in the mass is hardly more articulate than the lava over-flowing from a volcano. Like the volcano, this destructive force is always liable to erupt, one of the most terrifying and unacceptable 'acts of God'.

As we observe only too frequently in the second half of the twentieth century, language, in that finally degraded form, still plays a part. We are sharing in the break-down of a culture, the culture of Western man, the white man, as it has evolved hitherto through the migrations from the Middle East during the past

several millennia—three thousand, ten thousand years? It has
been a seamy, blood-soaked process, whose general trend
through predatory greed and cunning has made the moments of
spiritual ascendency seem to be only the more miraculous,
through the agency of individuals of genius in one or other of
the fields necessary to a civilisation; religion, science, mechanics,
politics, the arts, all of them demanding the fertilising magic
of words.

That genius has worked, also, through the quiet functions of
anonymous folk, whose gentleness, patience, humility, generation after generation, have ploughed the wilderness, built and
maintained the home, the village, the city, adding with coralline
persistence to the structure of an increasingly civil way of life,
with law, justice and sensitive definition of moral and aesthetic
values, all of this activity hardly openly expressive above the
grade of folk-art, but pure in that respect; elemental, fundamental.

So, with its masters and its servants, articulate in their degree,
this Western culture has grown. Two world wars, with the
parallel upheavals caused by population growths, the tumour of
the machine, and all the other unexpected phenomena of our
times, have cracked that culture like a Greek vase when the
crude excavations of equalitarian spades plunge in.

As society collapses under the assault, so too the arts reflecting
it are shattered. According to our age, our sensibility, our mental
and emotional predilection, we react to this racial drama, for or
against. It is impossible to be neutral, for the process is all-
embracing, touching the whole of mankind in the universal
displacement. It is larger than politics, vaster even than religious
consciousness and faith. It consumes even the latter-day sciences
which have served it. Its strange simplicity, a kind of new
infantilism, is dreadful because of its unassailable innocence.

A symbol of this force whose newness I am trying to isolate is
seen in the incident of the return of the American spacemen
from their circuits of the moon. As soon as they were brought

down to the decks of the aircraft carriers on the oceans of Mother Earth—they were presented with baseball caps! The implications of that gesture are manifold. It is a birth-pang articulation of a new way of life, in which the mystery and dignity of the Word has momentarily been left behind, because of its ramifications into the soil of the past.

The function of the poet today is to restore that mystery, that dignity. For without the Word, the future evolution of man must be towards an antlike, microscopic efficiency within the adventure of the species, silent and inexorable, in the transmigration to the planets. It will be another expulsion from the Garden of Innocence, but on a cosmic scale.

Meanwhile, the dignity, the grandeur of contemporary achievement, are deliberately ignored, and even denied. The heroes are given baseball caps, not Triumphal Arches, not Pyramids or Temples. All such symbols of perpetuation through the future centuries are regarded as the toys of superstition. The journey to the moon is treated as a team-job of technical co-operation. The individuals concerned are subordinated, and only moderately acclaimed by an organised understatement in which they themselves share. No Homer celebrates their endurance, their conquest. They put on the un-magic helmets of the baseball uniform, and are at once reduced to the level of the playboy.

What does this signify? Is it a new form of Puritanism, whose disciplines are based on the imaginative limits of the majority, that Demos which, because of its long history of subjection and slavery, now repudiates all reverence for the master-mind, and acclaims only its own exemplars, the pop-singer, the TV comedian, the professional ball-game star? This modern way of life, gregarious and equalitarian, must contain no mystery, no hierophant, no King-God, no hero.

I would not say, however, that this is a new thing. Heroes, leaders, have always been temporary, and have had to pay the price for their short ascendency. The opening paragraphs of Frazer's *The Golden Bough* picture the ceremony of the deposition and slaughter of a chief by his ordained successor. 'A candidate for the priesthood could only succeed to office by slaying the priest, and having slain him, he retained office till he was himself slain by a stronger or a craftier.'

It is a process of all social organisms, from that of the herds of cattle and deer to modern democracy. We deny the god-concept today by shortening the periods of acclamation. The leader has to be here today and gone tomorrow, and who can deny that this mass-cynicism, so openly displayed in the Americas, does not tend to save mankind from the horrors of tyranny, Stalin's being the last and worst?

The oligarchies which have now taken over may have brought social and political freedom a little nearer. They have also released the subconscious desire for revenge (a slave mentality) which is taking the form of a destructive nihilism comparable again to the conduct of the animal world—this time, the swarms of locusts in their all-devouring flights. This is more than a political matter. It is more than a social matter. It refers deeper to the disciplines of articulation, the painfully slow evolution of modes of self-expression which sublimate these dark mysteries and terrors of primeval life-force.

First among them, because of its utility value, is language. And it is through the gradual refinement of language, by the architecture of grammar, into the more sensitive modes of verbal music, the internal onomatopoeia by which the words used approach the otherwise indescribable and incommunicable awarenesses of the isolated human spirit, that civilisation is maintained and advanced.

The danger today is that we are substituting for language another medium, the alphabet of mathematics, on the false assumption that its symbols are absolute. They are not. They are propositions assumed as axioms, almost as remote in their origins as the roots of language. Bertrand Russell, a mathematician of genius, after a long life-work of practice in that medium, has said in his autobiography that this is so; that he has followed a chimera as uncertain as those of the priest and the poet. But he is wrong in being uncertain. That may be due to his following Leibnitz rather than the divine-visioned Spinoza, in whose concept of 'Substance' we can lose ourselves with confidence, reassured of finding ourselves again.

The achievements of mathematics, however, are dominant in the world today, and their authority is due to their cleanliness and mechanical accuracy. We are at present worshipping according to that direction. The machine, the computer, have advanced with astounding rapidity towards a degree that simulates selfconsciousness, and we bow down before this idol. For it is an idol, just as the icon, the many-armed, many-headed oriental figures, the sphinxes and pyramids, are idols, before whom mankind has bowed down, often in suicidal sacrifice, despite the warning of that more ulterior mystery and authority, language, the Word. 'Thou shalt have no other Gods but me', said the Word which that spiritual genius, the writer of the Fourth Gospel, proclaimed to 'be in the Beginning'.

What is that Beginning? Mathematics has not yet equated the answer, though the physicists are hopeful, following up Einstein's amazing simplification of the problem. But is not the rationality of mathematics being discarded in the process? Are not its classical principles, so aseptic in pure intellectuality, maintained since the days of Pythagoras, now restricting it to a materialism that makes it a coldly cruel god, as dangerous as the ancient gods of emotional blood-lust and animal vitality?

Can language be absolved from a similar accusation?

8

I believe it can, and my belief is based on a faith which dawned in my mind like a superb sunrise at the end of another seven years, when I was a boy of fourteen.

By that time I had read my way through the fiction departments of the public libraries in Battersea and Dulwich with the voracity of a mouse in a mealsack; the voracity and also the rodent unappreciativeness. I lived in my reading as I lived in the rest of my waking hours, unconsciously, but storing up mental ammunition. The process was slow. I must have been a late developer; or maybe the medium of language, which was to be the instrument that later would choose me as one of *its* instruments (again, life's paradoxes at work!), is different in its structure from the more isolated media, such as mine.

I think often of the prodigious activities of composers and painters. Their faculties spring fully equipped into their hands and minds. Mozart composed at the age of five. Berlioz wrote an octet when he was twelve, and in a non-musical, medical household. Raphael, Turner, Bonnington: they groped from the cradle and grasped a mature technique.

But a writer has to wait longer. I am not sure why, but I suspect that it is because his medium of language is also the daily, utilitarian means of communication, so primitive and instinctive a tool that it is almost wholly buried in the subconscious, like breathing. But we know that even breathing can be recognised, made a controlled, disciplined process if it is to serve a more determined purpose by the athlete, the orator, the singer, the actor; all of them, by necessity, making an art out of an instinct.

But breathing and using language are not so immediately noticeable to the immature mind as are the signs and symbols of the other arts, and of mathematics. These are more removed from daily need. They are, therefore, more conspicuous and palpable. If an infant receives them at all, he takes them wholly, and instantly.

This may be special pleading, an effort to find an excuse for my slowness in coming to the first stage of using language as an art, consciously and with a recognition of its deeper, more spiritually persuasive values, comparable to the overtone that hovers over bell-music, the sublimation of the octave.

But with language this sublimation is more than the extension of sound-waves, though indeed sound is one ingredient of this higher endowment. What was the drawback, the reluctance, of language in its use as a medium for art, delaying the young person's approach to it, proves later to be the treasury of inherited experience, history, wisdom, whose wealth makes every word an ingot of almost incalculable specific gravity, a rarer metal than gold.

This, the latent content of words is incalculable because it is being added to by daily usufruct, or compressed and hidden under desuetude. Custom, verbal fashion, changes the accepted meaning of words, slightly or sometimes completely. Some words are lost, except in the dictionary. Others are freshly coined either by a poet, an engineer, or a chemist. Some are borrowed or stolen from other languages, defaced and newly minted. An artist using language is like the afflicted Laocöon handling serpents. The German critic Lessing, friend of Goethe, used the Laocöon as a symbol for his massive study of the agonies of aesthetics. They beset the writer insidiously because they are caused by the *everydayness* of language, of words. The medium is rubbed, distorted, defiled. It is current in the market place, the brothel, and on the hustings. It poisons the lips that use it. It is abominable.

But it is also everything that is human, and of the society of man. It goes further, into the 'dark backward and abysm' which was even anterior to time. We know of this authority. We have accepted the idea that the Word is an epitome of the Creator made flesh. Christ is called *the Word*. That tremendous symbol cannot be dismissed even by the positive-minded atheist. It is a deep-rooted perennially vernal concept, which defeats while it enables that atheist to argue his case for a mechanical universe.

The Word came first. Mark Twain put the matter humorously when he wrote about Adam and Eve naming the animals. Eve called one of them the Dodo. 'But why', asked rational Adam, 'do you call it the Dodo?' Eve referred to a deeper knowledge, 'Because,' she said, 'it looks like a Dodo.'

It is the obscurations of familiarity which have to be dispersed by the writer before he can begin to master the medium of language. He has to learn, in the same necessity, so much about the history, the social content of words, and this is a task that adds to grammatical knowledge, a knowledge of people, their comings and goings, their commerce and chicane, their nobility and bestiality. He has, therefore, to become sophisticated in an adult way within the verbal terms of the community of which he is a contemporary. It is a slow process, concurrent with his daily, yearly experience.

But what about the naive achievements in the art of language; the folksong, the products of that astonishing artist *Anonymous*? What about the lyrical upthrust of young poets, who like their counterpart the young mathematicians, pour out their song, or their equations, with Shelley's skylark, from a full heart 'in unpremeditated art'?

That ever-occurring phenomenon would appear to contradict what I have stated to be a necessity for the writer, the slow maturing of a knowledge of social and natural environment and its condensation into the historical structure of language. It would be an obvious untruth to say that writing, as an art, is an occupation limited to adults.

My own experience gives the lie to such an absurd idea. I look back over sixty years to the second stage of my adventure with words and find it even less explicable than the first, which I have attempted in this book, and in the first volume of an autobiography, to describe. What I have succeeded in capturing is merely the factual happening, the sudden act of reading fluently, at the age of seven.

The second stage revealed itself when I was fourteen, during the penultimate year of my schooling at Dulwich Hamlet village school. I recall that school as an inspiring academy. It stood in open fields off the centre of the village, and looked across to a beautiful Georgian house built sideways to the road. I can still see the huge willow tree in the playground, and Beech House beyond it, with long windows, rose-red brickwork, chimney-stacks that woke my boyish imagination to vague cravings and appreciations. Yet that little school, which I was to leave at fifteen, a year later in 1908, was called an elementary school. I remember the headmaster, a short, thickset man whose name was Hunt. He once told the class that he hoped he was descended from a namesake who had been Shakespeare's usher at Stratford-on-Avon. The suggestion lodged in my mind like a grain of millet-seed. It created a living link. A few days later I furtively opened a tattered copy of *The Tempest*, hiding it under the desk because the class was supposed to be working on a card of problems in arithmetic, a too-frequent period which was sheer boredom to me.

I entered *The Tempest* at Act I, Scene 2, upon those yellow sands where Ariel, that Warwickshire Ganymede, induced the meeting of Ferdinand and Miranda.

The Mischief sang:

> Come unto these yellow sands,
> And then take hands:
> Courtsied when you have, and kiss'd
> The wild waves whist:
> Foot it featly here and there;
> And, sweet sprites, the burthen bear.

Everyone knows what followed. Three centuries of enraptured youth, and veterans too, have become innured to the enchantment. But that moment was my first awakening to it, and when Ferdinand whispered, awestricken

> Where should this music be? i' the air, or th' earth?

the anguished enquiry was mine also.

I read on, below the pretence of solving the arithmetical problem about water running into and out of a tank of stated dimensions, and I heard Ferdinand again voice my own bewilderment:

> This is no mortal business, nor the sound
> That the earth owes . . .

I can remember being angry with myself, and, panic-stricken, trying to brush the tears from my eyes without being noticed by my desk-companion, or the master, or any of the healthy, derisive urchins who provide the major population of school-rooms all around the world.

Something strange, some deep organic metamorphosis, was happening to me. I sat there, stone-still, but struggling to get out of that confinement. I read on further and came to Prospero's pretended threat to Ferdinand

> I'll manacle thy neck and feet together:
> Sea-water shalt thou drink; thy food shall be
> The fresh-brook mussels, wither'd roots, and husks
> Wherein the acorn cradled.

Again the music, the sound of the vowels and consonants, surged over me, like the surf on those 'yellow sands'. It made me suddenly aware and suspicious, as though I had found a nugget of gold there. I glared suspiciously around the classroom, daring my schoolmates to grab my find.

This is not an imagined scene, knocked up like a theatre backcloth by a hardened old professional. It is an actuality. It happened on a summer afternoon in 1907, a slumbrous moment in the schoolroom, with boredom and stifled resentment in the

D

air, because of the time being wasted there while the sunshine, the smell of cut grass, the puerile craving for movement, combined in vain to lure me away from those cards of problems in arithmetic.

But my disturbance was no more lethal than the shipwreck about which Prospero reassured his daughter.

> I have with such provision in mine art
> So safely ordered, that there is no soil,
> No, not so much perdition as an hair,
> Betid to any creature in the vessel
> Which thou heard'st cry, which thou saw'st sink.

I came back to my surroundings as unscathed as the Burning Bush in which the Divine Fire settled in order to illuminate the mind of Moses. But there was a warmth about me that did not subside. It made me feel physically lighter. I walked on air as I made my way home that afternoon. Everything looked more clean-cut; more sharply outlined. I remember that visual impression so vividly. It was as though the lenses in my spectacles had been strengthened. I can feel still the flush in my cheeks. The temperature of the universe had risen.

9

Mystics and theologians have had much to say about the number seven. It chimes through the Talmud and the Bible. It stands as illuminant on altars. Medieval biology stated that seven years is the term within which the whole cellular fabric of the animal body is renewed. The Gnostics, and after them the Rosicrucians, believed that the human body is not equipped with a soul until it is seven years old.

What does all this signify? Is it no more than a primeval superstition? Even so, the idea on which these concepts and practices are based is common to all mankind, at whatever stage of evolution a tribe or a culture may be. Week by seven-day week offer evidence of this fundamental concept, the mystery and holiness of the number seven. It touches the humanist (that latter-day Corinthian) as well as the devout worshipper of a conceived and accepted God.

So when I was seven my body and mind took on a new dimension. Again, when I was twice-seven yet another dimension was added to my consciousness. Maybe it is from this moment of enlargement that terms of measurement, implying the confinement of time and space, are exposed as artificial propositions that have to be discarded once the mind perceives reality.

Astro-physics appears to have reached such a stage of development today. Even that outsize ruler the 'light-year' is being discarded, along with the subdivisions of the millimetre under our inquisitions through the modern microscope. Inward and outward alike, we recognise infinity.

So science and mysticism, climbing through the centuries, by separate paths up the mountain of Understanding, appear to be approaching each other, only to agree that there is no summit to crown their undimensional pursuit. Having come nearer together, however, they may evolve an agreed teminology to express what is timeless and spaceless, this reality which is both here and there; then, now and to be.

All such concepts, by metaphor and paradox in language, by transcendental measurement in science, would serve my purpose, if I had the power and ability to command them, in trying to understand and define what was taking place, what was being created, in that schoolboy's personality, his whole ordinary but mysterious self, body, brain and 'x' the unknowable, in his fourteenth year.

I can only persist in my effort to be objective. I can only describe what happened, and take for granted the miracle of memory, and its invisible mechanism, which the Greeks deified as Mnemosyne, mother of the Muses.

Within a few weeks of that sleepy summer afternoon in the village schoolroom, when I looked up from Shakespeare's verse in *The Tempest* and saw the willow tree in the playground flaming with cold green fire under the sunlight, I asked my mother if I could have a table in my small bedroom, as I wanted to 'work' as well as sleep there.

She was one of those mothers who, constantly vigilant over their children, notice certain events and sayings and 'store these things up in their hearts'. That is archetypical of the perfect motherhood, and is recorded, therefore, in the story of Christ's life.

My mother looked at me, her warm brown eyes glinting enquiringly behind her gold-rimmed spectacles; but she asked no questions. She did not want to know what I meant by 'work'.

She was a school-teacher, but there was nothing professional in her relationship with her husband and her two sons, of which I was the younger and much less capable and intelligent. She was passionate, protective, but firm. On occasions she could deliver herself up to gaiety, but even in those moods her watchfulness against the world was never relaxed.

So I found the little table in my room, and on it a pen-tray, with a pen, a pencil and a bottle of Stephen's ink. She had provided all this and no word said. I accepted this clerical furniture as a matter of course. That is the way of a child towards its parents.

One of the many ornaments in our sitting-room was the folio-sized family bible, in thick, embossed covers, on which lay a circular d'oyley, crocheted by my mother. For the first time in my life, I became aware of it, purloined it from under the d'oyley, and took it up to my room. I did this with no deliberate purpose. The action might have been that of a sleep-walker. There the large, lugubrious volume lay on my little table, unopened, and again nothing was said by any of the three persons who comprised my universe, and from whom my semi-somnambulance was withdrawing me.

Then one night, with the first chill of approaching autumn in the air to bring foreboding, I opened the bible at the Book of Job, and began to read about the man 'in the land of Uz', who 'feared God and eschewed evil'. That word 'eschewed' hit me like a spark from an anvil. For the first time I saw a word as a concrete object, something to touch, to pick up and handle, feeling its shape, its texture, ringing it against my mind like a tuning-fork against anything hard, to listen to the vibrations and the tone.

I have just looked up that opening passage again, sixty-two years later, and I see that Job had seven sons and seven thousand sheep. Seven! It has taken a lifetime for me to spotlight that number. We move from ignorance, to certainty, to ignorance. If, in my noontide years, I knew what that 'seven' meant, I have lost it again in the evening twilight of my life. Like the boy of fourteen, I will let it pass, and go on, as he did, to a later passage that burned like a stigmatum into his memory.

That night I ruffled through the first eleven chapters, scattering the coloured syllables around me as I rushed on, delirious with excitement. I had no conception of the meaning of the debate between Job and his neighbours. They appeared to be criticising

him for being down-hearted, over the tribulations put upon
him by Satan after an experimental wager with God that this
good but privileged man could be brought so low by disaster
and sickness, that as Satan said 'he will curse Thee to thy face'.

Job's comforters, the prototypes of the 'I told you so' school,
had been picturesquely eloquent by the time they reached the
end of Chapter Eleven. Their eloquence was almost too much
for me. I was about to give up and stumble into bed, drunken
on this strong verbiage, when my eye alighted on a single phrase
in the next chapter: 'Doth not the ear try words?'

I read on, suddenly aware of what all this dialogue was about,
and that indeed this stricken man was *not* down-hearted, but
sustained, assured, powerfully armed. 'Surely I would speak to
the Almighty', cried Job. 'Hear diligently my speech, and my
declaration with your ears.' And after that the famous Chapter
Fourteen follows, like a great chorale by Handel, beginning
'Man that is born of woman is of few days, and full of trouble'.

All this, of course, is familiar, or at least *was* familiar, to a
community whose literacy and spiritual experience had for over
three centuries been drawn from the Bible, through the words
of the Authorised Version in which the poetic genius of Miles
Coverdale still flowered. Phrase by phrase, the metaphors had
been propounded and fed with commentary to the people from
Protestant pulpits, Sunday after Sunday.

But all that historical and episcopal dilution meant nothing to
me at that moment. I stood in a vast cathedral of sound, its
golden doors flung open and the music of this organic mixture
of medieval and Elizabethan prose-poetry throbbing and
tumbling round and round the newly perceived structure of my
mind. I actually had the illusion of my brain as a building conse-
crated to some purpose beyond my comprehension, but through
the authority, a divine one, of this tremendous power, the
Word.

What caused this revelation I believe, looking back over sixty
years at the experiences of my life, none of them a particularly

abnormal event, that I was at that time in an emotional state which made me open to such reception as I have tried to describe. I knew, by then, that the adored mother was ill. She had been ailing for two or three years. The visits by the local, suburban doctor, in his shabby hired brougham, with his ruffled top-hat and his black bag, had become more frequent. A backcloth of dread settled behind my schooldays, my excitements and those constant anticipations which are the waking consciousness, hour by hour of childhood. The ever-widening horizon was clouded, and I was silently, secretly, crying out for help.

In a miniature, puerile way I was in Job's plight. And like him I saw the doors open, and heard the command which he interpreted: 'Or speak to the earth, and it shall teach thee.'

Two years later I remembered that advice. It came with the sound of the handful of earth dropped on my mother's coffin in Highgate Cemetery, after it was lowered into her parents' grave.

In my bewildered anguish, to my guilty surprise, I found at that moment my mind wandering, and silently repeating, 'Doth not the ear try words?'

PART TWO
Touching the words

1

Now I fall into difficulties, because I must try to describe the experiences not even of an apprenticeship, but only the preliminary efforts and attractions to an apprenticeship. The ordinariness of such a period is baffling. It might bore a reader even if the apprenticeship were to a recognised skilled trade, such as watchmaking, or to gold- or silversmithing, which would command attention because of its speciality.

But to be apprenticed to the moulding and manipulating of words! It is almost a ridiculous suggestion, since everybody uses words daily, more or less fluently and sufficiently. The proposal might be compared with that of a student in one of our newer universities whose thesis for his Doctorate of Philosophy was 'Soccer'. Or we could go back to the activities of medieval theologians theorising upon the proportions of the Wafer, or the notorious conundrum about the number of angels capable of being accommodated on the point of a needle.

I have deliberately made that last sentence ponderous, in the manner of the pedant, wrapping up a worn-out cliché in circumlocution. This is the thing to avoid, especially in writing about experiences common to all human beings. And of those, the naive adventures and discoveries of the young, at the budding-time of their lives, are the most dangerous to touch because of their similarity. The post-war book world is clogged with autobiographies covering the period of childhood and youth. Some are written by artists skilful enough to transform the personal into the universal, and to touch it with magic. Most are written by sentimentalists, nostalgic over some private little corpses of yesterdays which they fail to bring to life. G. K. Chesterton was aware of this over-trodden track and of the probability that it might be a cul-de-sac. He wrote apologetically in his autobiography: 'I fear that I have prolonged preposterously this note on the nursery; as if I had been an unconscionable time, not dying but being born, or at least being brought up. Well, I believe in prolonging childhood . . .'

My purpose here in prolonging my discussion of the childhood of the mind is to avoid missing the miracle. Like the archeologist, I must move the mountain with a spoon and a tea-strainer for fear of losing the tiniest shard of that miracle. And my search is not philological, which is the scientific study of word-origins, grammar, rhetoric and even literary criticism (as some Cambridge pundits have claimed). Nor is my search wholly semantic, diving down through the ocean of time to discover the rock-bottom meaning of words.

I am after something which is more elusive because it is so ordinary, so commonplace. It may be connected, as the title of this book implies, with that extrasensory perception which is much under discussion by philosophers and psychologists today. Arnold Toynbee, in his book *Experiences*, writes of this elusive but ever-present communicant. He says that he discussed it with his friend Gilbert Murray, 'who possessed extrasensory perception in an unusually high degree, and held that, in varying degrees, it is possessed and is used by all human beings. His view was that, in a conversation, something more passes between the parties than is conveyed by the spoken word'.

What distinguishes creative literature from the mere mechanistics of utility language is that this 'something more' referred to by Gilbert Murray is also conveyed by the written word. In his little book, his credo called *Religio Grammatici*, he enlarges on this, and brings to the proof a statement of the sensibilities of a great Humanist who, like Toynbee too, was initiated into the fourth dimension of mystical reality by a secular but deeply religious willingness to accept the unacceptable.

Such a resolution is not rare, especially in our age of increasing literacy and expanding knowledge of the structure and nature of the universe; if it be a universe. But we have a new paradox today, since in spite of the discarding of positivism as an inadequate instrument in the search for the first cause both in ourselves and our surroundings, our sophisticated use of language, as Toynbee observes, 'is pushing extrasensory perception into the fringe'. Yet it is that perception which keeps language alive, both as symbol and manifest of the mystery which the human race, in its deeds as well as its sublimations, is for ever, and increasingly, trying to unveil.

2

At the time I made this discovery, more than sixty years ago, the name for it, 'extrasensory perception', was unknown to me. The currency of the psychologists was not so far-reaching in their trade amongst the markets of the mind. Like all currencies, that coinage is only a substitute for the real thing; no more than a promissory note. As we go through life we lay up the illusion of riches in this way, and are deceived by our various vocabularies (whether they be in words or any other medium) into the belief that we are secure in our solid possessions of knowledge, or whatever concrete form our possessions may take.

But one tremor of mind-quake can shatter the figment, and leave us with nothing, just as an earthquake can destroy a city. 'Words fail me'! How glibly that cliché comes upon the tongue in the trivial eventualities of life, a hundred times a day. But on the great occasions which we must all confront, disastrous or sublime, that exclamation becomes a fundamental and fateful truth. Most crises are moments of silence. Life, which itself is an utterance, is arrested while we are plunged into nothingness for the fraction of a second. But that fraction is an aspect of eternity.

This experience, however, is recognisable by man. In this he is unique amongst living organisms. At least, that is as far as we know today. Future research may reveal that an avalanche perceives its own descent, a volcano its own eruption, a mouse its own peril from a selfconscious cat. But that is not yet. We still believe mankind to be singular in the creation of arts, those instruments of paradox by which he bridges and records experiences, either objective or subjective, which are otherwise ineffable.

That is what I mean by 'touching the words'. The medium might be other than language. Milton, who was a musician as well as a poet, wrote of 'touching the tender stops of various quills'. Keats, in his *Ode on a Grecian Urn*, saw, and described, in the stilled figures of the festal procession round the vase, the symbolical capture of this arrested fraction of a moment in human consciousness in which the dreadful silence of the 'unheard music' is sweeter than the 'heard music'.

These are common certainties, frequenting every day, and known to every person. But they are cataclysmic, and they shelter certain assumptious, habits, conventions. They destroy us and renew us on a larger scale.

That scale is a clearer measurement of order, of proportion in whatever direction we look, either outward on our surroundings, or inward on our capacity. This is what the Greeks sought, through their *logos, logismos, arithmos* (word, geometry, number), synonymous with meditation, a practice on which Plato depended in his expansion of the use of memory, or recollection. The French naturalist J. H. Fabre wrote a poem aspostrophising that *Arithmos* (number). It begins:

> *Nombre, regulateur des effets et des causes,*
> *Qui donne le comment et le pourquoi des choses,*
> *Que me veut tu, Nombre imposant?*

'What do you demand of me, Number?' I would say, in the same spirit of awe, 'What do you demand of me, Word?' I have been uttering that negative prayer during my sixty years' apprenticeship to the *mystery* (as crafts were called in the Middle Ages) of the art of writing. The counsel and the purpose of that pursuit is to increase the practitioner's understanding, in depth beyond depth of allusion, of the words he is using. The glibness must be reduced, and the precision increased.

That, however, is an adult, an ultimate, aim. It is so exhausting, so elusive, that it usually leads us to silence, so that in old age we end where we began, as inarticulate in our mortuary retreat as when we made the first approach to the art, through the dawn of consciousness.

I am concerned now with that dawn, still trying to trace its colourful articulation over the sky of my mind. I see, but only dimly over the distance of the years, the schoolboy sitting at the little table in his bedroom, intoxicated by the verbal wine of that seventeenth-century English vintage, the Authorised Version of the Bible. His drunkenness was of the solemn kind. It made him silent, vague and grandiose. From that hour he called his bedroom his 'study', and saw himself as a Keatsian 'eremite'. The drug of syllables had taken possession of his puerile brain. Henceforth it 'had him in thrall'.

Those images from the poetry of John Keats are deliberately chosen, because the next step in my lifelong intoxication was the step obvious and usual with English writers since the mid-nineteenth century. I fell under the spell of the poetry written in the five years 1815 to 1820 by this feverish medical student who relinquished his intended profession in order to devote himself wholly to the pursuit in which I intended to follow him. Such was his fervour and endowment, that thousands of aspirants like myself have joined the procession. I believe many, at an early stage in their awakening, continue to do so, though the way of life and the imitative trend of culture in the second half of the twentieth century may have set up less rapturous models.

3

I have described, in a more intimately biographical book, the moment when the genius of John Keats confronted me like a divine visitation. It coincided with one of those experiences so common in the minds of adolescents, when depression and a vague, cosmic foreboding descends on the young person, who is just about to embark on those 'strange seas of thought, alone', unaware that not only Newton but almost every mortal soul has undertaken that voyage.

This *weltschmerz* which is the seedling of much of human arts and religions was given a closer focus at that time by illness in the family. The adored mother was fading, and we knew it. I, so desperately attached to her because of persistent childhood ailments, was now her nurse, forced to be morbidly precocious in clinical duties that should have been a woman's job.

On that particular day my brother, my elder monitor, was also in bed, sick and irritable after an attack of influenza. He too was concerned with the nearing future, the need to qualify for some way of earning a living. In 1908 there were no Welfare State, and very few scholarships. Children of the minor civil servant and the elementary school-teacher, with no *legitimate* family tradition, or any connection with the competitive world of business, could not conceive of a safe means of livelihood other than by following in their parents' petty professions. To work at a trade, a craft, or as an artist, was believed to be wholly impossible. It was to court starvation. Risk was almost synonymous with crime. So too was any activity connected principally with money-making. At that age, and in that miniscule environment, I remember that I considered the idea with a vague dread and disgust. I associated banks, stockbrokers, 'the City', with horse-racing and other gambling procedures.

So with misery and boredom both my brother and I 'swotted'

E

to take examinations that would qualify him to be another elementary school-teacher and me another minor civil servant, salaried and assured ultimately of modest pensions. No other way of life was conceivable in our small family rectangle.

Both boys loathed the necessity, for my brother was already a gifted musician, with an astonishing faculty for reading a score straight, while I sat at odd, snatched moments in that 'study' which I have already described, where I brooded between the duties of sick-nursing and the dread of watching the surrender of the mother who was the centre of my emotional life. I groped vaguely towards some other orientation still intangible, and tainted because of my sense of disloyalty towards my dying mother.

Thus, surrounded by these morbid shadows, I nevertheless lived my days, urged on by some curious power of sub-assurance, some intimation of destiny for which I still cannot account.

On that morning I prepared the midday meal for the permanent and the temporary invalids. I was free for this domestic ministry because I had left the elementary school after taking an examination for a post in the lowest grade of the Civil Service, in which I should begin a career in the same way as did Josiah Stamp (later a distinguished financier), and my contemporary W. J. Brown (later the founder of a civil servants' union, and an Independent Member of Parliament). I was then fifteen, and had completed my official 'education'.

The interregnum, between leaving school and learning the result of the examination which was to make me safe for life from the threat of starvation or the degradation of going into the 'business world', enabled me to run the household.

My father was at work and my brother going daily to a training college. Mother's failing powers induced a minor problem. She refused to have a woman in the house. I could not understand why: nor did I question her mania. I imagined that we could not afford the wages, for she was no longer earning

£110 a year as a teacher in a slum school in Battersea, where doubtless she had contracted the illness which was destroying her, as I realised every time I emptied the little basin of blood and mucous, or held her shoulders and breasts while her body was racked with bouts of coughing and fighting for breath.

I had served her lunch that morning, after burning 'asthma cure' powder in her room to prevent an attack during the meal. Then I took up a tray to my brother, who was now sitting up in bed, convalescent but impatient. The bed was littered with music scores and books. He had discovered an affinity for the late nineteenth-century French composers: Debussy, Fauré, Ravel. They gave him a secret delight, and he played their music with awed reverence on our Klingmann pianoforte (made in Berlin), which Mother, by superhuman contriving, had bought for him some years earlier.

He accepted the tray, pushing some books aside for me to place it across his knees. One book fell to the floor, and I picked it up. It was a selection of the poems of John Keats, covered in red leather with a swallow outlined in gilt on the front.

While my brother was eating the grilled chop, I lingered in his room. He was the kind of person who attracts people to him and remains silent, content with that rewarding approach. I was hungry too, and rather weary after the domestic chores. But the emanation of personality from my brother warmed me with an invisible sustenance, and I opened the book, perhaps merely to avoid the embarrassment felt when one person is eating and the other is not. My attention alighted, like a butterfly on a flower, at the opening line of a poem which later in my literary life I was to be troubled by because of its youthful naivety and lapses in taste. The line was

I stood tiptoe upon a little hill . . .

Then something happened: a flash of blinding light, an augury, a prophecy.

I have described this adventure in my earlier autobiographical book, and need not repeat my attempt. But I did not remark on the aptness of Keats's imagery to my own situation. At that time I too was standing tiptoe lifting myself above myself in a kind of *ecstasia*, the intoxication seeping in through every pore of my mental skin. The metaphor is deliberately mixed, to suggest the confusion of mind and senses in that ardour of adolescence. Every object around me was both magnified and clarified, under a strange, intense illumination.

But this alpine-treading, this glorious ascent, took place after all on the 'little hill' of my local environment, the wooded and beflowered London suburb, Dulwich Village.

It was a sacred hill to me at that time, still almost rural and quiet. It was associated, too, with this other world into which I had just stumbled: the magical world of words. The air that swayed the elm trees in the village street was full of incantations, for had not Edward Alleyn walked there, owned the land, built the old 'College of God's Gift'? And had he not been an associate of Shakespeare, a boy-actor in the plays, probably taken the part of Miranda and mouthed aloud for the first time those words which had enraptured the young Ferdinand as well as the schoolboy furtively reading them under the cover of the schoolroom desk when he was supposed to be solving problems in arithmetic?

> There's nothing ill can dwell in such a temple:
> If the ill spirit have so fair a house,
> Good things will strive to dwell with't.

I too shared that inexperienced girl's belief. In spite of the dread and foreboding caused by family life in a household of sickness, and in an environment demanding the acceptance of economic slavery, I saw my surroundings as 'so fair a house' that I was uplifted to a state of expectant delirium. A shapely cup in my hand, a sprig of honeysuckle in our diminutive garden, a momentary cessation of my mother's suffering, all could touch me into this state of wonder and worship.

On this material base there rose the structure of my new awareness: the form, the sound, the juxtaposing of syllables, the interplay of vowel and consonant. I was drawn within the word.

4

Was this a morbid condition, due to the particular and almost pathological circumstances of my years of puberty? Was that *fin de siècle* period, the Edwardian drag-out of the tremendous achievement of the nineteenth century in Europe, a decadent environment contributing to my feverish development?

The first decade of the twentieth century was ugly. It produced nothing of aesthetic distinction. The ascendency of the costing-clerk over the craftsman had begun. The machine-made, mass-produced article was still clumsily imitative of the manual. Where there had been wrought iron there was now cast iron. And the cast iron clamped down on the articulation of an expanding society, holding it still in the rusting framework of feudalism. So the new, brash and clumsy, conspired with the old, effete and rigid, to frustrate the emergence of a social organism for which a few prophets, artists and statesmen were striving at that time.

I believe there was nothing unique in my condition or in my environment during those years of awakening. Youth has always been so. Circumstances, as a closer look at the history of mankind shows, have always preoccupied the young. The seed of those certainties lies in every individual born into this world, whether in the caves of prehistoric man, the Athens of Pericles, the Jerusalem of Claudius, the gaudy filth of Gloriana's England, or the concrete camps of our contemporary international self-service equality.

The potential rebels against this ever-threatening social environment, with its perverse mis-direction, are always being born, as freely as millet-seed. But, like that seed, the majority is lost in the humus of circumstance. Only here and there a few fecundate and feed on the decay which is the ground-base of growth and material evolution.

Those few rebels are the articulate ones, the finders of a means of expression that is constructive, harmonising and unifying towards a future way of life still beyond our present comprehension. They work in moral, scientific, and artistic experiment, each to his bent, but sharing a common purpose.

The means of that sharing is the Word. Without it, the probing genius of man is likely to lose its way, to become isolated, one technique contra another at a chance meeting. Language, even though fractionalised at the time of the punitive erection of the Tower of Babel, is the distinction of man. It is the instrument for bringing his activities together as a creative purpose, simple and therefore of universal articulation.

It can also be a dangerous instrument, like a gun in the hands of a madman. We know the consequences of its abuse today by the commercial ascendency of the newspapers and magazines, and all the wiles and exaggerations of the verbal media of advertising.

Language can minister to disease as well as to wisdom. I think of John Ruskin, one of my first literary heroes because my home in Herne Hill at the threshold of Dulwich, stood at the bottom of a hill-lane at that time shaded by a grove of black poplar trees and aspens, that whispered incessantly through the leafy seasons. The lane was called Ruskin Walk, and it emerged on to Herne Hill almost opposite the house where Ruskin spent his boyhood, an only child imprisoned in the care of rich, insanely possessive parents who warped his manhood, wrecked his marriage, and overstrained the genius which later degenerated from authoritative aesthetic perception and pronouncement, into eccentricity—finally madness.

This grandeur, and its wreckage, were reflected in his prose. At its best, it had a virile rhythm that carried ideas and sensations simultaneously like an accumulation of sunlit clouds, moving in a stately splendour more aerial than any prose paragraphs in English since the days of its infancy when Chaucer wrote his treatise on the Astrolabe, or the later masters in the seventeenth century, Milton, Fuller, Jeremy Taylor, gave the prose paragraph a musical unfolding equating with poetry.

Yet, towards the end of his life, on the occasion of a revisit to the scenes of his childhood in Dulwich, he could use his literary powers to fulminate as follows:

But, for its sense or fancy, what food, or stimulus, can it find in that foul causeway of its youthful pilgrimage? What would have happened to myself, so directed, I cannot clearly imagine. Possibly, I might have got interested in the old iron and wood-shavings and become an engineer or a carpenter: but for the children of today, accustomed from the instant they are out of their cradles to the sight of this infinite nastiness, prevailing as a fixed condition of the universe, over the face of nature, and accompanying all the operations of industrious man, what is to be the scholastic issue? Unless, indeed, the thrill of scientific vanity in the primary analysis of some unheard-of process of corruption—or the reward of microscopic research in the sight of worms with more legs, and achari of more curious generation than ever vivified the more simply smelling plasma of antiquity.

It is a sad sight to see that 'achari' as Ruskin called it, the over-flowering of a passion-tormented imagination, producing such a paragraph to describe the change of the rural Croxted Lane of his childhood walks into the suburban residential road which he had just revisited in old age. That was in 1880. What verbal catastrophe would have erupted from him if he returned today, to find that Croxted Lane no longer 'separated by blackberry hedges from the better-cared-for meadows on each side of it; growing more weeds, therefore, than they, and perhaps in spring a primrose or two—white archangel—daisies plenty, and purple thistles in autumn'?

I have picked on this aberration because it is so closely associated, geographically, with my own experience and development in the use of language. To find the feet of clay on which so many of our former gods once stood, warns us of our own tendency to top-heavy superstructure. I ask myself if, in this curious enquiry into language, I may be labouring the obvious commonplace; making much ado about nothing. The materialist and the cynic would certainly say so. But there is no justification for such a dismissal. Any self-criticism of my essay is not that I am overdoing the theme, but that I lack the knowledge, the sensibility and the imaginative penetration to handle it rewardingly.

Rutherford and Cockcroft, at work to release the secret of the atom, may easily have been compared with an infant chasing a butterfly. I am not sure in what degree I stand between those extremes of purpose, the scientific sophisticates, and the puerile naturalist. Are they all destructive in their efforts, and I in mine? Would it not be safer to *use*, rather than to *dissect*?

I cannot answer my own query. Here I come to a standstill, with my enquiries conjured around me. I am a child who has taken an old familiar clock to pieces and is at a loss how to put them together again, none the wiser about the significance of each separate piece of the comparatively simple machine. What shall I do with the cog-wheels of words, now that I have begun to question their derivation and use? Most people know that even to take one word, out of everyday and unthinking repetition, to think about it, examine it, even merely to question the way it is spelled, is to find it vanishing into meaninglessness, nothingness, like one in a foreign and unknown tongue.

5

But we can approach though we do not understand, as the infant, to its peril, approaches the fire. The unknown arouses curiosity, the most persistent motive power in life. Curiosity summons the other positive forces: courage, persistence, constructive imitativeness, and all the other tools in our armoury towards mastering the unknown, and thereby building a civilisation. At least it supplies the mechanics for that purpose, as reverence supplies the morals.

I remember the sensation of peril which tempered my boyish excitement when I first consciously approached words, the digits of my native language. They suddenly took on admonitory firmness. They became monumental, and I passed among them as through an avenue of weathered statues, chiselled, in a past beyond my comprehension, by vanished masons. Accompanying the ecstasy which I have tried to describe, a feeling of awe, of fear, disturbed me. It affected me physically. I felt a fluttering sensation in the centre of my body, the diaphragm. I still feel it, every day when I sit down to face a virgin page of paper, and for a few moments the spasm has a paralysing control over my mind. I wait, as submissive and, I might admit, as dishonest as a medium in a trance, for the transmission to come through: dishonest because the process is not under the control of rational thought, of laborious planning. Something other than that admirable and sane authority puts the opening words to paper, and it causes a time-lapse before intellectual conscience can take over, to keep the flow of words under control, drilling them into the intention of required meaning, and the rhythms of justified persuasion.

We are all dishonest in so far as we have to disguise, at every endeavour, our uncertainty about our equipment to face a certain situation. And that occurs every day, maybe every hour of our lives. Primitive warriors were taught to shout and scream as a necessary disguise, to hide this dishonesty, both from the enemy and from themselves. It is a bridging movement, over an abyss of irresolution. It fills the moment before that of contact with the Goliath of circumstances.

But there has to be something stable in our characters, behind this momentary 'dishonesty', this self-deception of assumed courage. It is a deeper-rooted quality, closer by affinity to the mysterious beginnings of the authority of language. The poet John Keats, in one of those precociously mature letters to his brother, called this quality the power of 'negative capability'. It is a latent force, and is thus parellel to and in harmony with the fundamental nature of words. It is a patience, a faith, a serene confidence during the dark suspension of clear thought, and it *knows*, though with no guarantee, that all will be well.

In another of his letters Keats tries again to define this condition of relaxed control in the conscious mind. He refers to

> the World or Elemental Space suited for the proper action of Mind and Heart on each other for the purpose of forming the Soul or Intelligence destined to possess the sense of Identity. I can scarcely express what I but dimly perceive—and yet I think I perceive it. I will call the world a School instituted for the purpose of teaching little children to read—I will call the human heart the horn Book used in that School, and I will call the Child able to read, the Soul made from that School and its horn Book. . . . Not merely is the Heart a Horn-book. It is the Mind's Bible, it is the Mind's experience, it is the Text from which the Mind or Intelligence sucks its identity.

All this is metaphysical, but it is also grasping at reality, and in terms of the mystery of language, which is also my purpose in this enquiry into the point of junction where human life and language meet.

6

They met for me in those tempestuous months of puberty, that stage of life when the young person is publicly seen to struggle out of the confinements of childhood, as a snake out of its first skin. My reading habits took on a new fervour. The excitement of the narrative continued, but it was now a candle-flame after sunrise. I was blinded by the incandescent orb of language.

My intelligence suffered. I ought to have been soberly absorbing facts, the academic fodder that would sustain me in the examination rooms of the Civil Service Commission, towards which my common sense and my family tradition were directing me, inexorably and without my questioning that grey destiny.

Enthusiasm is a word much debated since it was first used by the Greeks to name a state of spiritual intoxication, when a human being is visited by a god, and recognises the visitor. So it is a word in the dictionary of religious experience. We know the risks involved. They have been fully explored by poets, historians, theologians, since the story of mankind began to be recorded. In general, the consequence of enthusiasm had been deemed to be tragedy. Homer, Aeschylus, Sophocles, Euripides, made that association of the two words, enthusiasm and tragedy, an inevitable binary.

Every mythology, each with its special theology, is a theme with variations on this belief that the mortal whom a god visits, is doomed to disaster because of the imposition put upon his frail mortality. It may be the crushing burden of foresight (think of what befell Prometheus!). It may be an increased access of aftersight, of interpretative wisdom. It may be a propulsion into the fourth dimension of extrasensory experience. It is always suspect in the society of his fellow men, for it affects his conduct in such a way that he is no longer one with those fellow men. He does the irrational thing, the unexpected thing.

He breaks the taboo, and becomes an outcast. In a superb, a splendid, a cosmic way, he is a drunkard, thrown into the village impound until he is sober.

But enthusiasm is a stronger intoxicant than wine. If it works upon a mortal, and then departs, it leaves behind a depleted wretch who too frequently tries to revive that glory by turning to the minor and still more temporary stimulant. The biographies of people possessed by genius (which is another manifest of enthusiasm) are monotonous with this anticlimax, the fall into alcoholism after the genius has flared out.

Or if the enthusiasm persists it becomes a haunting demon who drives the limited human brain and nervous system beyond breaking point, as it did with Ruskin and Jonathan Swift, John Clare and Christopher Smart, Hölderlin and Schumann, irretrievably and finally. Often it induced temporary alienation, as in Shelley's fits of somnolence and erotic hysteria, Byron's outbreaks of sadistic rage, Leopardi's melancholy. The examples are legion among the immortals in every walk of life.

Can one blame the philosopher John Locke, that early guide to the sobriety of the Welfare State, for saying 'enthusiasm is founded neither on reason nor divine revelation, but rises from the conceits of a warmed or overweening imagination'?

His suspicion of this visitation was shared by the Victorian J. A. Froude, who believed that 'resolutions adopted in enthusiasm are often repented of when excitement has been succeeded by the wearing duties of hard everyday routine'.

That was not my experience. I was to be submitted to 'the wearing duties of hard everyday routine' in the Civil Service for twenty-four years before I dared to abandon myself to the siren voices of the enthusiasm which sang to me that day at my brother's bedside and never died away in the corridors and offices of Whitehall. At the age of forty, life's sober noonday, I could resist them no longer, and I abandoned social and financial safety to follow them, and to give myself wholly to this 'enthusiasm' which Locke and Froude so flat-footedly misinterpreted.

How I contrived to pass the entrance examination that made me a 'permanent' civil servant I do not know. My mental and emotional diet at that time was almost wholly this preoccupation with words, through the poetry of the English and French Romantics, and, later, that of Edmund Spenser and Milton. These last two drove me mad. I waded through *The Faerie Queene*, bored and confused by the allegory, enchanted by the versification with its lacework of epithet. I found those 'sea-shouldering whales' which Keats had followed in his own sensuous practice. I stared at the crest on the gentle knight's helmet 'like to an almond-tree mounted high'. I remember that I came upon that image while returning to my lonely suburban rooms standing in a crowded London County Council tramcar, swaying as it shrieked and moaned over the worn rails along the sordid Walworth Road. But the magic of that phrase 'like to an almond tree' dispelled the rising nausea of tram-sickness, and gave my end-of-day solitude a rich comfort and companionship, beyond the scope of Locke's reason, and Froude's stove-pipe-hatted sobriety.

7

Circumstances, and perhaps some inherited respect for the decorum of my Victorian forbears, prevented me from repudiating completely the legalistic council of Messrs. Locke and Froude. I knew that I had to earn my living, and I felt no inclination to the Bohemianism affected by so many of the fringe members of the world of the arts, and so few of the master practitioners.

Maybe the fact that my parents were sympathetic as well as sensible about my first and lasting love-affair, the infatuation with words, led me to agree with their persuasion that I should find myself a secure niche in the economic world, which in those days appeared to be so stable, though severely graduated. At sixteen I became a civil servant in a legal department called the Land Registry. I found myself amongst a set of lawyers and a tradition of precise language.

This environment offered a healthy counter-balance to my giddy excitement, the logomania which so dangerously had raised my mental and even my physical temperature. To my gratification (though being still a child I accepted all as a matter of course) those lawyers took an amused interest in my mania. Thus my formal education continued, and I was practical-minded enough to take advantage of it. When my mother died in the year after that of my entering the Land Registry, one of those legal officers, named John Stewart-Wallace, took over the proving of her will and offered me a spiritual kindness which prevented my shaken universe from crashing. Only two weeks before her death she had given me a birthday present, the works of Lord Macaulay in seven volumes of the Everyman Library. I bought the books one lunchtime and stood them on my table in the Registry. Mr. Stewart-Wallace passed through, saw the pile of books, and stopped to examine them. He also examined me, with a shrewd but kindly eye. That led to some enquiry about my interests in life, what I did with my time, what my plans were towards a career. I remember telling him solemnly that I proposed to be a poet.

I still can recall the pause that followed, and the closer scrutiny of my juvenile person, only too patent behind my spectacles. Then he said, with an equal solemnity that must have been assumed, 'You must not, however, take Macaulay as a model if you are to be a poet. I would rather recommend Milton.'

Further monitoring of this kind followed during the twelve months, until in 1911 I was transferred, after passing another ghastly examination, to the Government Laboratory, where I continued to do clerical work, but amid a set of chemists. These also were graduates of universities, and valuable to me as stabilising influences while I rushed headlong on my chosen way.

Thirty years later I was by chance to meet Sir John Stewart-Wallace aboard ship, and to accept his invitation to lecture in London at a meeting of the World Congress of Faiths, of which he was chairman. My theme was 'The Element of Faith in Literature'. It is really the theme of this little book, in which I am trying to discover why so ordinary and everyday exercise as language is a miraculous bridge into the Unknown, something we all exploit as persistently as the air we breathe, and with as scanty gratitude.

The Government Laboratory became my substitute for both grammar school and university. The lawyers had insisted on precision in the choice of words. The chemists added a discipline in the use of facts. In addition to these official matters, these superiorly educated men appreciated my efforts to explore, in solitude, the whole continent of knowledge and its reflection in the arts. Thus, as I went along, I created my own tutorial system while earning my living in the world at large, and thus I avoided the dangers of the cloister, to which the more formal academic environments are prone.

Perhaps the most valuable part of the terms spent at a university is that environment, which by osmotic penetration educates the student in practice and quality, which he receives subconsciously, or rather supra-consciously, in parallel with the theory, the bookwork.

During the whole of my years in the Civil Service I had this receptive advantage; the discipline of contact with men trained to think impersonally, and to express their thoughts economically. In general, also, the world of our British Civil Service was then less competitive than that of business and politics. This made the relationship between us comparable to that of students at a university, a rivalry towards perfection in work, rather than personal advantage. That was the atmosphere, though of course the clarity of it was occasionally befogged by human nature, as in all mortal institutions.

In the second half of my twenty-four years in the Civil Service I worked in Whitehall at the headquarters of the Ministry of Labour, and there was in contact with men of still more varied cultural range. Among my colleagues were Alan Barlow, a classical scholar, Humbert Wolfe, a poet, C. K. Munro, a dramatist, C. E. M. Joad, a loquacious expositor of philosophy, John Hilton, an economist; all of them consciously aware of the mystery of words, and of its disciplinary demands.

What more could I need than such daily company, in addition to that of the larger and more average humanity which provides the rank and file of all gigantic organisations, the salt, but also the roughage, of the earth? This was as bracing as being out in the mid-ocean of human society. So I had the cultural encouragement of Oxford or Cambridge, without their cloistral conceits, those vocational diseases which caused Hilaire Belloc to describe their victims as 'remote and ineffectual'. But he spoke nearly three-quarters of a century ago. The dons have ventured out since then, to help in the waging of wars, the administering of governmental policies, and the scientific development

F

of industry. That is not the only change in the academic field! Some of the wreckage of the cultural revolution of the second half of the twentieth century has been littered even there.

8

Those first years, when I began to earn what I believed to be a secure living, were sparse enough, for I began at the bottom of the official grades. The economics and domestic aspects of that status I have already described elsewhere, both in autobiography and fiction.

I have not, however, plunged deeper into an exploration of the mental and emotional activities by which I sought and fought my way into the craft of writing. This is a much harder task, as I have already shown in these hesitant pages.

The logomania, the fever of words, whose virus entered my blood on that memorable if somewhat morbid day when I stood by my brother's bedside and read what appears to be a not notably inspired line of Keats's verse, was not reduced in the chilly wards of the Civil Service, where I was to be enclosed daily for so many years.

After the death of my mother my father married again and the home was dispersed. My brother and I lived in rooms for a while, then he too married, and I was left alone. Contact with humanity was mainly during office hours. My free time was spent in the solitude of my rooms, and thus I was able to do more reading than most undergraduates. My fervour whipped me into a discipline that became routine. I got up at five o'clock every morning, read for two hours, then bathed and breakfasted, to leave at 8.15 for the Government Laboratory, where I put in a seven-hour day. I was back in my rooms by five in the afternoon, having stopped on the way to buy a bloater or a pair of kippers for the evening meal.

I read during that meal, having begrudged the minutes spent in preparing it. I read on through the evening until midnight, surrounded by lamplight and silence in winter; suburban footsteps, voices and other street noises in summer. I was elsewhere whatever the season. Like the boy Coleridge, stopped by a constable in the Strand because he was proceeding suspectably waving his arms and breathing to excess, I could say that 'I was swimming the Hellespont'.

I had not yet learned to discriminate. At that time the opiate poetry of Francis Thompson had spilled over from the literary field into the world at large. It was quoted in pulpits. I fell under the spell of those lush verses, as disturbed youngsters today consume cannabis. Thompson's muse strode over my mind 'and left the flushed print in a poppy there'. He sang

> Hearken my chant, 'tis
> As a Bacchante's;
> Flown vaunt 'tis,

and I hearkened, intoxicated by the outrageous rhymes and the lurid excess of imagery. Here indeed was a verbal foliage to touch, and tremble at because of the spiritual sensuality it implied, the phrases contradicting the religious intent.

Fortunately, the cautionary suggestion by the lawyer in the Land Registry a year earlier had not been disregarded. I had looked into the rather dreary Victorian edition of Milton's poems (it had been a school prize awarded to my mother), and though at first repelled by the appalling dignity of the verse, I soon began to realise that here was a command of words unparalleled by any other practitioners in the English language.

Years later, T. S. Eliot (with whom I was to be associated in friendship and as a contributor, under his editorship, to *The Criterion*) severely castigated Milton for his puritanical influence on the free flow of English prosody.

But I heard in those early years, as I still hear today, the summons of that perfect placing of syllables, the resolution of vowel sounds, the percussion of consonants, as this deceptively austere master musician called to me

> O'er the smooth emerald green
> Where no print of step hath been,

Follow me as I sing,
And touch the warbled string.
Under the shady roof
Of branching Elm Star proof,
Follow me.
I will bring you where she sits
Clad in splendour as befits
Her deity.
Such a rural Queen
All Arcadia hath not seen.

Is it unexpected that this tremendous personality, equipped with wide-ranging scholarship and an immaculate technique, so musically excellent, should almost overwhelm the boy, struggling by instinct rather than by monitorship to educate himself in this art? Milton reduced me to humility with his admonition to 'strictly meditate the thankless Muse'. I could not understand, in my innocence, what Milton meant by 'thankless Muse'. Now, sixty years later, I know, only too ruefully, but gratefully. I have learned that all nine of Mnemosyne's daughters are both thankless and elusive, coming and going capriciously among their human suitors, since they are free of a larger acquaintance than we mortals can comprise, within our consciousness so clumsily limited by the instruments of the flesh.

But the flesh implies senses, the five senses which include touch, that primary contact beginning with a groping blindly for the nipple. It can be developed through the finger-tips of an executive musician, an eye-surgeon, a painter and a craftsman. It can be symbolical, as in my present effort to show the young, embryonic writer feeling his way towards words, not so much intellectually as sensuously, as I imagine a sculptor feels with his hands the stone or wood which he intends to shape into an image of nature, or even some subjective shape embodying a private aesthetic experience.

In some respects this preliminary reaching out, this touching of the medium, is a fear-engendered indulgence, a means of delaying action and decision. It is nostalgic in reverse; a *longing towards* future attack and achievement. So much depends on that shy approach to the material, that sensuous contact with it, that subconscious testing of its texture, its mass, its pliability.

It has all the potentiality of ignorance and hope, of that cloudy ambition which later must be reduced and solidified under the dictation and authority of the material chosen as the vehicle of this venture to express the mystery and beauty of life, and make them both static and immortal, a sublime contradiction.

> For ever warm and still to be enjoyed,
> For ever panting and for ever young;
> All breathing human passion far above . . .

But the 'breathing human passion' goes into the task of making a work of art, after previously hovering, like a pregnant woman's mind over the foetus in her womb, round the medium in which the new creation is to be embodied.

Such a concept of the approach to the beginnings of a vocation, in any walk of life, is likely to be dismissed with contempt today. Our ideas about first and last things are so much conditioned by mechanistic practice. Even the achievement of carrying man to the moon is made a process of engineering, of accumulated scientific articulations. No mysticism, no symbolism, are referred to. Those spacemen, and the army of instrumentalists and calculators on the ground, are not consciously challenging the gods, as did Daedalus and his unfortunate son. We have another terminology in the latter half of the twentieth century, and it is being applied also to our explorations in philosophy and aesthetics. But superstition persists because the horizons of the universe remain elusive, like those nine Muses. And superstition sits at the doorstep to knowledge. Old idols, old myths, are abandoned, but we see the newer instruments being worshipped. The computer has its priests. It is only a more accurate, useful and responsive form of the Golden Calf.

But little is advanced by rejection, and I believe that in trying to understand the beginnings of any life-process, especially those of the human consciousness in its moments of first recognitions, there should be no dismissal of terminologies, either traditional or individually eccentric, since life itself once took an evolutionary step thereby, and, as Milton said in his essay on freedom of thought and expression: ' 'Tis true, no age can restore a life, whereof perhaps there is no great loss; and revolutions of ages do not oft recover the loss of a rejected truth, for the want of which whole nations fare the worse.'

9

Thus, swimming against the tide of contemporary fashion in the arts, criticism, morals, and general way of life, I still hold my faith in the melodic line, the Aristotelean assertion that art should be 'an imitation of nature', thereby giving our subjective urge a recognisable shape within some objective form. I believe that without this faith, and the disciplined practice it ensures, man is doomed to his own private fantasy, and the human race to insanity and extinction.

But no young person believes in extinction, unless he is hopelessly diseased by mental illness or drugs. Young arteries, young veins, are flooded with the ichor from the powerhouse of hope, of curiosity, of a healthy self-assertion in a universe newly created, in an environment of surprise and wondering acclamation. Even the melancholy and languors of adolescence are no more than impatience while waiting for the curtain to rise on this tremendous drama of life.

This vitality governs the tyro's handling of whatever medium he is led to adopt. The beginner, in eagerness, does everything to excess. He has yet to learn restraint, the imposition of method, the need to isolate the object whose characteristics have excited his passion, so that he may enhance it within a frame, the process of art.

So even with the exemplary art of Spenser and Milton, grave, but lavish; religious, but verbally sensual, to be the principal textures attracting my touch, to feel the magical threads along the fabric of words, I could not control more extravagant youthful gestures. I was groping everywhere in the twilight of my own dawn.

Of course, Keats was an inevitable attraction; his poems and from his poems to his letters; all prodigious in beauty and their humane wisdom. And Shelley, historically associated with Keats but diametrically opposite, drew me almost irritably because the

speed of his verse made me giddy. At that time I saw its faults;
the loose, defective texture of his verse, a lack of quality which
later in life I found in the prose of Aldous Huxley. It is an
unlikely defect in two men whose genius was of the same kind,
deeply religious yet revolutionary and sceptical, inclined to
impractical crankiness yet scientific in intellectual interests.
Shelley had no time to mature, as did Huxley through a more
profound discipline of experience. But speculation is endless,
and of little use, in what Keats, Shelley and Byron might have
done had they not died young. There they shine in the firmament,
a triune constellation unique in its tragic myth

> For ever panting and for ever young.

and likely to attract beginners perennially because of that
premature arrest.

Shelley's versification offers a wealth of examples of what may
be called word-fixations, but for the fact that the words which
he over-used were always symbols of velocity, of bodilessness.
*Liquid: flowing: streams: fountains; azure: aerial: echo; speed:
melting: starry.* His vocabulary was large because of his great
intellectual capacity, but it was inflated with words that reflected
his temperament. He was always about to take off from solid
earth, in spite of his fundamental ballast of humane sanity. That
was why Matthew Arnold made the wrong judgment by calling
him 'an ineffectual angel'. Browning was nearer the truth by
saluting him as 'sun-treader'.

These niceties were not observed by the young newcomer. My
appetite was too voracious to be selective. And before appeasing
my hunger, before even picking, I had to touch the fruit in the
orchards of English and French literature, words beyond words.
There stood the great masters, each a singular tree of astounding
fecundity, and amongst them a host of dubious bushes, bearing
softer and ephemeral fruits. I was dumb, confronted with such
excess. I had no words of my own.

PART THREE
Moving and placing the words

1

In childhood I had wakened to words; in youth I reached out, curious in my hunger to touch them. All was tentative, hesitant. That could not last. Hunger must be appeased, and like a young scientist in a lavishly equipped laboratory I had to start experimenting, with no particular proposition or theorem in mind.

That was the time, of course, to have settled down to close academic study during the customary three years in Oxford or Cambridge University. But in my life hitherto such a training had been an impossible dream, if dreamed at all.

In the teens of the twentieth century only a combination of good health, a powerful intellect, and self-sacrificing parents, enabled a child to take one of the rare scholarships to a grammar school, and thence by the same process to a university. That path was well trodden through the centuries. Cardinal Wolsey took it. So did the poet Christopher Marlowe.

Unfortunately, I lacked both the physical and intellectual vigour in childhood to follow that path, and the opportunity lost during those few essential years could not be retrieved. I was in a worse case than Shakespeare, who 'had little Latin and less Greek'. I had no Latin and no Greek.

Given my passion for words, why did I not subsequently make up for this deficiency? It was because the passion was abnormal. It raised my temperature, and drove me to wayward procedures, all of them feverish over those years at the threshold of manhood when mental discipline and guidance are most imperative.

My discipline was naive and home-made. It was based on whim rather than wisdom. Only a character of great intellectual endowment can be wise at eighteen. I lacked the intellectual endowment, the powerful memory, the far-seeing gift of reasoning. I had to rely on nervous sensibility, a fragile instrument, especially when lodged in a febrile body. But we all have our handicaps, one of the most dangerous of which is self-pity.

It is good to discover them, however, at an early stage in one's life, so that some sort of compensation may be established.

I have described how fortunate I was during my adolescent years in the Civil Service by finding monitorship in older and more socially and academically sophisticated colleagues, first in the Land Registry, then in the Government Laboratory, where in all I spent eleven years before going on to the Ministry of Labour in Whitehall, known in 1920 as 'the nest of singing birds' because Humbert Wolfe, a Deputy Secretary as well as poet, was collecting round him a staff of men and women with tastes and predilections similar to his own. His theory was that if a person were sensitive and expressive enough to be interested in any of the arts he was likely to be a lively and imaginative official, unfettered by too much bureaucratic caution and *laisser-faire*. I am not sure that the theory was practicable. It did not allow for the fact that 'a man cannot serve two masters'. I suspect that was why, in my case, it tended to an incurable imbalance. And that is an understatement.

Certainly in the early years of my government service my monomania for words interfered with my efforts to become a useful official. I never fully developed that way because throughout the period of apprenticeship I was in the throes of this infatuation. Bernard Shaw said that a poet was a man who would remorselessly convert his mother's milk into printer's ink. If the Civil Service can be described, by some insane hyperbole, as maternal, then I would apply Shaw's witticism to my relationship with the three government departments in which I served. Promotions were no true reflection of it. The many friendships and literary encouragements found there merely disguised my divided loyalties.

The years of reading and imitative writing in solitude during my hours away from the office so fixed me in habitual practice that even marriage and family life could not break it.

I bought little notebooks, at tuppence a time, bound in black waterproof and sturdy enough to be carried in my pocket. Every day I made a list of words newly discovered in my reading, or snatched curiously at random from the dictionary. I wrote them down in those notebooks, with their meaning and origins, and memorised them as a child memorises the multiplication tables. I moved them about in my mind, walking the streets, riding in London tramcars, cycling into Kent or further afield. I put them into verses, and took them out again to adorn prose paragraphs.

In my reading I was more concerned to observe how the masters had used my ever-growing collection of words than to deepen my consciousness of what those masters meant, and what bearing their writings had on the matter in hand: life, death, our senses, our passions, and the oscillations of the social machine. I was hardly aware of the existence of the social machine, although I had become a cog in the wheels of its elaborate administrative set-up.

Thus my state of mind during that period devoted to moving words about was a form of insanity comparable to that of any other person with a mania for collecting, whatever the objects might be: postage stamps, pictures, porcelain, matchbox lids, sea-shells, or any other of the perishable currency with which we mortals deceive ourselves between the poverty of birth and the poverty of death.

I sought my vocabulary in the most ornamental of writers, the Elizabethans, the magnificent word-mongers of the seventeenth and eighteenth centuries, the Romantics and moralists of the nineteenth. I did not mind the admonition of Sir Thomas Browne, the physician of Norwich, that 'the iniquity of oblivion blindly scattereth her poppy, and deals with the memory of men without distinction to merit of perpetuity'.

I studied this master's prose as though I were analysing the setting of a jewelled brooch. I could read even the following passage without being brought up short by its dire warning: 'to hope for eternity by enigmatical epithets or first letters of our names, to be studied by antiquaries, who we were, and have new names given us like many of the mummies, are cold consolations unto the students of perpetuity, even by everlasting languages'.

I could not believe, even had I paused to doubt, that those 'everlasting languages' are as ephemeral as any other changing organism, merely by being a living phenomenon. I believed words to be absolute, noumenal. That mistake is a pitiable example of the plight of the lone seeker, the hermit scholar, of whom in that untidy era of the Industrial Age there were thousands in our cities, and hundreds in our countryside, as indeed there had been throughout the history of mankind, before our latter-day explosion of pseudo-literacy, which has compelled governments to organise scalable education systems, from Brooklyn to Harvard, from Battersea to Balliol.

Even the substance of the Authorised Version of the Bible, as I have already shown, was only secondary to my attention to the words, that pile of post-Elizabethan grandeur imposed upon the poetic contribution of Miles Coverdale. Children reared in our Technological Age, who read the Bible (if they read it at all) in the new journalese version laboriously signposted by recognisable cliché find the Jacobean richness of metaphor as incomprehensible as Samurian hieroglyphs, though only a century ago that prose was the hornbook of every local preacher, trade-union leader, and village school-marm.

Even that vast authority on which our English-speaking cultural life was founded was used by me as an archeologist uses a long-barrow or other site. I collected and studied words as though they were shards or fragments of mosaic, tangible evidences of ways of life wholly unknown to me.

I had yet to become interested in the ways of life so copiously represented by language. I was hardly even aware that I was myself part of the present way of life so actively moulding new isotopes of the words which I was pinning down in my little black notebooks and in my memory, unaware that the usage of those words in everyday life was in continual if gradual flux. Thus I was in danger of condemning myself to pedantry, as probably may be seen by a younger, modernist reader of this book. But our verbal wear, like our clothes, our manners, and other social techniques, become part of ourselves, and we do well not to mind how they distinguish us, even though they lag behind the latest mode, or make us be derided as living anachronisms.

G

2

The habit of memorising my private and capricious dictionaries in the little black notebooks led me, almost unconsciously, to repeating the words aloud, either in the solitude of my rooms or the greater loneliness of the streets on my way to and from work. I often noticed that passersby glanced at me either with alarm or amusement, suspecting what is now called a 'nut case'. I did not mind. I was armoured by the magisterial self-possession of the extremely shy: another example of nature's paradoxes.

I tramped daily over London Bridge, closed in the early-morning phalanx, hardly able to swing my arms, so close were the ranks of the dragooned workers, surging into the City. But I was concerned with my little, incoherent Collect for the Day; one page from the little black book, revised again after compilation.

This method inevitably led me to give first importance to the sound of the words so randomly rehearsed. This attraction was further emphasised because my interest in music was constantly stimulated by my brother, whose influence over me, a life-long force, was not diminished by his marriage and removal to another domestic setting, nor by his early death. I set up syllables like sheets of notation, and thus their tone and timing became displayed within imaginary staves to my inward ear, through the fusion of the two attributes of sight and sound.

It is difficult to describe this expansion of word-consciousness without sounding extravagant and eccentric. But young people need to be extravagant and eccentric. Nature makes them so, as part of the process of growth. In the overcrowded and over-standardised society of our State-controlled twentieth century this natural power still breaks bounds, either destructively and blindly by mob protest, or savingly for the individual character by a passive withdrawal. The reaction was already in practice sixty years ago, before the First World War, as indeed it was when young Joseph, that Old Testament flower-child with the coat of many colours, withdrew himself from the herd-habits of his elder brothers, to suffer, but to gain a profitable exile.

So, by making an overheard music of my hoarded words, I began to move them with a great sense of pattern and vocal contrast. I also began, again instinctively, to read the work of authors who, like Milton, were linguistic musicians. I found both example and precept in Thomas de Quincey. He prided himself on his pronunciation when reading aloud:

> If I had any vanity at all connected with any endowment or attainment of mine, it was with this; for I had observed that no accomplishment was so rare. . . . People in general either read poetry without any passion at all, or else overstep the modesty of nature, and read not like scholars. Of late, if I have felt moved by anything in books, it has been by the grand lamentations of *Samson Agonistes*, or the great harmonies of the Satanic speeches in *Paradise Regained*, when read aloud by myself. A young lady sometimes comes and drinks tea with us: at her request and M–'s I now and then read W–'s poems to them. (W–, by the by, is the only poet I ever met who could read his own verses; often indeed he reads admirably.)

That reference to Wordsworth did not arrest me at the time, for I had not yet come to the deeper significance of words, an experience I hope to reveal in the last section of this book. Other personal records of contact with Wordsworth, as for instance that of Crabb Robinson, the man-about-town in literary England at that time, refer to the poet's Lake District accent, a dialect that survived a professional family setting and a Cambridge education.

Nowadays, dialects are hidden away in the cupboards of childhood, by people who have 'got on' in the world, and come south to the metropolis. This meaningless form of minor snobbery is a loss to the richness and variety of the English language. Few writers have dared to perpetuate dialect as literature, making 'a great verse unto a little clan'. Outstanding among them Robert Burns, William Barnes, and Hugh Mac-Diarmid, are likely to preserve these regional accents and vocabularies long after the dialect has otherwise disappeared.

I was unfortunate in being London-born outside the ranks of the real Costers who, like all city-bred illiterates, make a folk-art of under-slung, abbreviated syllables, twanged with adenoidal irony, swift and barbed.

The flattening of vowels and the elision of consonants appear to be characteristic of urban-bred larynxes, and this malformation is common to all dialects debased by crowded city life. It is heard in London, Dublin, Glasgow and Edinburgh. Yet the trained and cultivated pronunciation in these cities is English at its best, undistorted by the selfconscious specialisations imported by the class snobbery of some public schools and some Oxford and Cambridge colleges. These specialisations, however, are almost extinct, driven out by the craving to be deemed democratic, and the dread of being stigmatised as what used to be called 'posh'.

That word is rarely heard in England in the 1960s, and only by people of the older generations. It is an example of slang, probably a corruption of 'polish', and by association with smartness was used to describe highly cleaned articles but also well-turned-out persons, including their other attributes, such as speech, social standing and manners, and aristocratic birth.

The word 'aristocrat' is also becoming a period piece. A century ago it was used literally, and acceptably, by a class-conscious community, to describe a 'nobility or privileged class', the titled landowning families. The word cloaked the frequently dubious morality of those family histories, and the characters and conduct of their scions. It carried an overtone of respect for these people, whatever their individual worth. The 'aristocrat' was 'posh'. The concept had about it an affinity with the idea of 'divine right', that claim which proved so fatal to our Stuart kings, but is so deep-rooted in the past, down to the structures of tribal aboriginality (as Frazer showed in *The Golden Bough*) that it continues to decorate our social symbolism, even in a democratic age.

But now that democracy is in the ascendency, and is stripping the aristocracy of their wealth by means of death-duties and other taxation, seizing their estates and noble country mansions for public use and exploitation, the old respect, after passing through a phase of envious hatred (sometimes justified), has given place to an amused acceptance, comparable to the attitude of the French Republic towards its Two Hundred titled families, ghostly survivors of the Feudal System and the monstrous rule of the Bourbons.

So the word 'aristocrat' today carries neither reverence nor opprobrium, when issuing, so rarely, from the lips of the younger generation. Reverence instead is given to the self-made millionaire, and opprobrium to the omniverous State. The change of direction only emphasises the reality that what commands the interest and subservience of people is money and the power that money bestows. The word *aristocrat* is fading away, with the upper and exclusive stratum of society for which it stood.

But it is capable of revival. Words are like comets. They can recede in orbit by some unaccountable ellipsis, and return on another plane, with different connotations and social reference. To speak today of anything or anybody being 'aristocratic' is to evoke its first and classical meaning of 'rule by the best, the virtuous', and we conjure up, maybe subconsciously, the quality of purity, cleanness of line, a sort of Platonic selectiveness of breed, of form, fastidious in its austerity and avoidance of extravagant ornament. It has become an aesthetic rather than a social concept, and more rightly so than when used in connection with the exclusive nobility who, down the centuries, claimed it, along with so much else of which their persons and practices were so undeserving.

Such a word, so nobly and anciently generated, cannot die

like shallow-rooted slang. No other can replace it, and people who still value virtue, style, purity in all aspects of life, mental, moral, physical, find again and again that this definition, *aristocratic*, occurs in their conversation and writing, riding like the moon through the breaking clouds of resentment and hatred inevitably engendered by the majority of our people, descendants of the serfs of the feudal countryside, and of the underpaid factory workers in the early and crude industrial conurbations so rapidly inflated, and likely to be as rapidly erased.

So also, with such short-lived phases of social change under the urgency of industrial and technological evolution, the swollen population, with its semi-literate cultural values, the slang-words invented as short-term definitions of mechanical objects and processes, will be reduced to a more stable structure, economically and culturally, with the added advantage of the miraculous mobility which our physicists and engineers evolved almost overnight in the middle decades of the twentieth century, to the confusion of our politics, our morals, our domestic values and manners.

3

The confusion in my adolescent ploy of shifting words about, after my first discovery of them by reading, and the more deliberate collection of them in my little black notebooks, coincided with the confusion, on a vast scale, of my environment. Western society at that time was in the state of tumescence that erupted into the 1914–18 war, the first phase of the world-wide revolution which is likely to disturb the whole human race for at least the remainder of the twentieth century.

This racial upheaval is reflected in our arts; both their form and content. The reflection is no new thing, nor is it undesirable. Aristotle's dictum that 'art is an imitation of nature' is funda-mental, but it is more than gnomic: it carries oracular inter-pretations of that word 'nature'. They are infinite, and behind them all is the reverent mind of a man of scientific genius, one of mankind's first empiricists, who saw *nature* as the eternally revealable manifest of a central design, a coherence, a logic, which reappeared in the mysterious opening phrases of the Fourth Gospel: 'In the beginning was the Word, and the Word was with God, and the Word was God. The same was in the beginning with God.'

So Aristotle's allusion to *nature* was no mere pantheism, nor was Spinoza's allusion to 'substance', two thousand years later. Both philosophers had the same vision of an organic unit, existing beyond the bounds of even our present human concepts of time and space, existing and functioning according to laws equally beyond our understanding. We erect traditions of religious consciousness, of scientific analysis, of artistic presen-tation, as aids to expand that understanding.

Western art, until the explosion of all accepted values and relationships in the twentieth century, has tended to an almost literal acceptance of Aristotle's definitions. The arts have tried, with increasing actuality, to represent 'nature', which has been accepted as meaning our earthly environment. Even our religious, Christian symbolism has been embodied materially.

That representation of things around us reached such perfection that it became a kind of 'art for art's sake', concerned with technical accuracy. Artists in all media—stone, paint, language—have despaired of further development in that direction. They could not see how to advance beyond what has already been done, under this limited interpretation of Aristotle's dictum. The Greek sculptors, and the masters of the Renaissance, had done all there was to do. The poets of Europe had said all there was to say, by direct statement, and an imagery related to recognisable phenomena.

That despair was already seeping into the Western arts at the end of the nineteenth century. Certain practitioners were turning to the non-representational abstractions of Oriental traditions; the cryptic enigmas of Chinese poetry, the elaborate symbolism of the Persian rug-makers, the psychological disciplines of Jewish theology, which forbade efforts to *embody* in art either deity or mortal.

From representation, our arts turned to more esoteric symbols, and admitted the adventures of personal caprice in this pursuit. Mallarmé wrote poetry that deliberately broke the rules of classical form and patent meaning. We know what followed that breakage. The world wars, the rise of the proletariats, the mingling of races through accelerated transport, new political and economic ideas infused with social conscience unrelated to theological dogmas, all these influences came flooding in on the tide of science and technology. The breach was complete. The building we call Tradition, collapsed. The hungry generations of today, floundering in the flood, revile the ruins.

4

Chaos in human relationships and in the social culture based on them is equivalent to a vacuum in nature. Neither can last, but in the instant aftermath the rush of forces to fill the vacuum makes 'chaos worse confounded'. Since the world wars, all manner of splinter groups have been formed, and are still being formed, out of fragments of the ruins of our cultural and our religious institutions, by which tradition was formerly maintained. And the uncertainty of those groups, movements, creeds, has produced a vast amount of pretentious theorising, like the advertising campaigns of specious and even fraudulent business concerns.

The word 'permissive' describes them all. Our whole mid-century society, so far as it can be called a society, has named itself 'permissive', and done so with unction, with self-congratulation. Walt Whitman predicted such a state of mind a century ago (during the American Civil War): 'Do I contradict myself? Very well, then I contradict myself!'

That applies to us today, both to the individual and to the community. We see this so-called freedom of the masses of mankind being claimed and partially enacted, by peoples more and more enslaved within the State, which enriches itself by monopoly and taxation. As populations grow, so the States, in order to keep control of the hysteria of overcrowded human nature, penetrate by cancerous legislation into the life of the individual; his domestic habits, his education, his choice of work and play, and, through all these, his self-expression by means of words.

A dreadful sameness threatens us, due to the necessary standardisation organised by governments with the co-operation of economists and scientific technicians. Capitalist and Communist states are bound to become indistinguishable from each other, except by their means of coercion, as populations grow.

So, amid wreckage of the past, and the conglomerate re-building towards a world-wide control of the human race, this welter of eccentricity, this *permissiveness*, adds a third bewilder-ment to the life of the individual in every aspect of his journey from the cradle to the grave: his personal taste, his moral code, his choice and range of experience, mental and physical.

But is this a new thing? Are some Jeremiahs justified in prophesying that it is the beginning of the end of human life on earth, with small probability of total racial emigration to any other planet? Towards the decadence of the Roman Empire, when conditions at the centre must have seemed equally deplor-able and beyond hope, the poet Horace cried out in defiance of the pessimists, in an apothegm which I have already quoted. His sentiment, though hardly admirable or heroic, was a signal of the power of survival. We have no comfortable assurance, however, that history repeats itself. The only factor that appears to be constant, amid ever-changing circumstances, is this mysterious ingredient in human nature which spoke up in Horace's outcry, as it had done centuries earlier through the afflictions of Job. It survives alongside the complaintive streak of pessimism which is heard, from time to time, especially on historical occasions of perilous crises, voicing a dark contradic-tion through all religious creeds, all philosophies, all individual personalities. It even moved the lips of Christ, before his tor-tured body expired on the Cross. Maybe that was the last-minute manifest of his humanity, before he resumed his god-head. Myth or miracle, that shadow has a permanent significance, expressed in words. '*Eloi, Eloi, lama sabachthani?*' ('My God! My God, why hast thou forsaken me?')

Whether that story be a myth, another version of the seem-ingly indestructible symbol of the mystery of supra-rational consciousness, with which mankind is so emphatically and disturbingly endowed, or whether it be fact exceptional to the known laws of nature, we recognise in those words at the final moment of Christ's mortal agony, an ironic gloss on the oracular statement at the opening of St. John's Gospel: 'In the beginning was the Word'. It was Matthew and Mark who credited Jesus with that exclamation of human weakness, and thereby brought the story more endearingly close to our earth-bound experience and capability.

Luke, the more sophisticated narrator, the doctor, said that the last words were 'Into thy hands I commend my spirit.' That offers another reference back to the mysterious saying about the Word being in the beginning. Christ having been a total embodiment of that Word, removes it to its more universal state, and without a record of reproach, no mandrake cry.

John himself, the mystic who introduced this elusive reference to the Word being in the Beginning (could be have heen learned in the teachings of Plato?), wrote that Christ's last words were 'It is finished'. That is both more abrupt and oracular. An utterance from Delphi or Eleusis could not be more evasive. But it links up with his opening sentence to deposit a Beginning and an End, if we interpret him literally. The whole purpose of this book is not to do so.

5

This is, however, dangerous. The positivist (if there be a person left with this limited superstition today) will at once dismiss my enquiry as mere religiosity. Even the humanist may be dismayed, and say that I am trying to sit on a fence that isn't there!

But the truth may live in the danger. That danger is due to the adventuring among contradictions, as they loom up, not only in logic but in life. The attempt to relate words to actuality is that adventure. It is part of the impossible effort to deduce philosophy from the events of history. This problem has teased thinking man since he first began to record experience and his reflections upon it. The problem is an emotive one, based on our craving to see a pattern in all phenomena, from the structure and functioning of nature, to the directive consciousness of super-nature.

The key to that problem is this elusive and mysterious claim, for the authority of the Word. Those Gospels to which I have dared to refer, proclaim this authority, the three by implication, and the fourth by a direct poetic statement of it. The Word, which is consciousness, universally immanent and pervasive, is embodied in this figure, the humanised Christ. The concept is a step forward in evolution, the vision of a genius looking towards unity. The contention of all prophets, all artists, and all scientists, so far as they are working in first-hand contact with the manifest of reality around them, is that there must be a pattern of cause and effect, ever continuous, of which time and space are only measurements limited to the capacity of man's mind.

In that belief, the fourth part of my enquiry into the nature of words will concern itself with their responsibility in the propor-tions and articulations of human goings-on. I realise that many people today deny the evidence of this coherence, this pattern, in the shape and functioning of the universe. They see nothing but episodes. The historian H. A. L. Fisher wrote his massive *History of Europe* in that belief, or lack of belief. I suspect that the philosophic theory of Existentialism has the same basis: that things are merely what they are, and we take only them here and now. Such an idea of dissociation, however, when put into a technical practice by the painter Seurat, in his method of *pointilism*, disproves itself by showing the factual paradox of here and now as also eternity, and therefore perpetual association. The end-product of Seurat's tiny points of colour is a suffusion of light, a new revelation of the spectrum of life itself, serene, close-fitting, as firm as the classical integrations of Ingres' static compositions.

Yet Seurat worked upon a scientific theory, as though he were trying to put into the technique of painting, the philosophic principles of Kierkegaard; trying to 'see God' by means of a microscopic intensity, rather than by a cosmic enlargement and the slow easements of experience. Both the artist and the philosopher succeeded, to the limit of human capability; but both died young. It may be fanciful to surmise that there is some possibility of cause and effect, between these two men's method of mental effort, and their premature death.

But the luminous beauty of Seurat's pictures, where the seemingly dissociated points of colour draw together with a kind of pulsating and unified animation, is a living example of the miraculous paradox by which the universe, including man with his mental and spiritual processes, functions and articulates.

6

Articulation, for man at least, has a particular reference to words. It brings me back to my own story, the effort to achieve ease and accuracy in self-expression, and beyond that, to arrest my own experiences in the flow of life, and thereby to give them permanence, like the figures on the Greek vase apostrophised by John Keats. It is a statement of faith, of life in death.

Art, and in particular the art that uses words, is therefore faith carried into proof. It brings life to a standstill, and thus posed in perpetual mobility before generation after generation, incidentally adding to the structure of civilisation, of tradition.

I call this essay 'my own story'; but is it so? Is it not a commonplace record of organic growth, the mechanics of the conscious mind nourishing itself upon physical experience which we call mortality, so general, so repetitive, that we may also call it fate? But for one exception, we might compare it with the life-cycle of the gnat, the ephemarid born to hum amid its monotonous myriads at sunrise and to die after dusk, with no other adventure.

That exception is the Word, and the interpretative faculty expressed by it. If our physical fingerprints are assurances of unique individuality, how much more unprecedented is the something, the spirit, within that unique body, struggling to show its reaction to those all too familiar experiences of mortal life; the hunger, fear, sex urge, and the other ramifications that occur and recur, the more deadeningly recognisable the older we grow?

That exception is the Word, which arms us with curiosity and expressiveness, making of everyday life a theme with variations: the theme, our environment; the variations, our vocational selves; vocational and vocal. As word-users, we each begin at the Beginning, since the Word is eternally primitive. It is a chemical not of this world, for it dissolves time and space. Even the modern physicists, mechanically devouring time and space to inhume the moon and planets, are nursed upon the Word. It is the mother-milk of human knowledge.

When we are young we take the Word for granted. Most of us remain young in this faculty, because it is seemingly so elementary, so vastly quantitative. 'Of the making of books, there is no end,' said Solomon nearly three thousand years ago. How infinitely more vast is the flood of words. Yet, upon examination, we find that the average citizen in a sophisticated society commands a vocabulary not much larger than that of a tribesman in the upper reaches of the Amazon. In a highly developed language the wealthy range is there, but few exploit it, or even know of it.

My reading of Milton and Shakespeare during those years of adolescence that were spent so much in solitude, and therefore with more than the usual introspection, made me recognise my own verbal confinement. It exasperated me. I beat upon the walls of my prison. The little black notebooks were my hammers.

The mechanical collecting and memorising of words was only a beginning. I began next to sort them out, gloating over them like a boy over his marbles. I moved them about, related them to each other in phrases, sentences, and later into verses and paragraphs. The consciousness of the shape of paragraphs came later, as I matured grammatically and began to appreciate the subtle musical structure of prose. I can remember, sixty years later, how the boy of sixteen, smooth-chinned and eager, gloated over the following passage from Milton's essay on *The Doctrine of Divorce*, entirely oblivious of the content of the paragraph, but working himself up into a state of feverish excitement over the powerful linking up, continuity and chromatic fullness of sound as the clauses throbbed through this masterly orchestration.

It is worth listening to that again. I can feel my skin tingle and my blood race in my veins, under the sensuous clamour of this word-music.

What thing more instituted to the solace and delight of man than marriage? And yet the misinterpreting of some scripture, directed mainly against the abusers of the law for divorce given by Moses, hath changed the blessing of matrimony not seldom into a familiar and coinhabiting mischief; at least into a drooping and disconsolate household captivity, without refuge or redemption. So ungoverned and so wild a race doth superstition run us, from one extreme of abused liberty into the other of unmerciful restraint. For although God in the first ordaining of marriage taught us to what end he did it, in words expressly implying the apt and cheerful conversation of man with woman, to comfort and refresh him against the evil of solitary life, not mentioning the purpose of generation till afterwards, as being but a secondary end in dignity, though not in necessity: yet now, if any two be but once handed in the church, and have tasted in any sort the nuptial bed, let them find themselves never so mistaken in their dispositions through any error, concealment, or misadventure, that through their different tempers, thoughts and constitutions, they can neither be to one another a remedy against loneliness, nor live in any union or contentment all their days; yet they shall, so they be but suitably weaponed to the least possibility of sensual enjoyment, be made, spite of antipathy, to fadge together, and combine as they may to their unspeakable wearisomeness, and despair of all sociable delight in the ordinance which God established to that very end. What a calamity is this? and, as the wise man, if he were alive, would sigh out in his own phrase, what a 'sore evil is this under the sun!'

If a journalist, at the top of his profession, were 'to sigh out in his own phrase' such a paragraph as that today his editor would carve it up mercilessly. Even a staid publisher would demur if he found it in the manuscript of a book by a famous divine or sociologist.

The architecture of English prose which could carry on a paragraph so massive and so weighty was to be relegated shortly after Milton wrote it. Dryden, followed by Addison, favoured a lighter framework, suited to a less ponderous readership as the news-sheets began to find a larger and less scholarly public. And with the ever-increasing public, so the prose has become less chromatic, discarding impressiveness in favour of utility and speed. It has had farther to go in the community, and cannot carry the weight of learning and aesthetic grandeur.

But an examination of Milton's build-up in that paragraph shows that its clauses, so dexterously marshalled between colon and semi-colon, cover the matter in hand with legal precision and provision, while adding a passionate musical urgency of movement, characteristic of that great word-organist who was later to perform more thunderously and sublimely in *Paradise Lost* and *Samson Agonistes*.

What amuses me now is the fact that I totally disregarded the contents of that essay when I read it so many years ago, attracted to it as blindly as a moth to the candle-flame, or as a sunflower writhing on its stalk to bask in the full glory of the sun. I cannot explain the attraction. At that age I was interested neither in marriage nor divorce. I had hardly heard of divorce, so happily enclosed was my Edwardian home-life.

But the disturbance of my mind was vigorous enough, as I took those phrases like fruit from the tree. I savoured their ripeness, and their disposition along the boughs. I was learning how to *move* words, how to arrange them to their fullest advantage. But the exercise was almost in a vacuum. I was bemused by a drug of syllables, and in this state I wandered off into a pedantry, a grammarian's world, probably not dissimilar in my auto-intoxication from the 'flower-children' who have opted out of the overwhelming social complexities and dreadful portent of the latter half of the twentieth century.

H

7

Grandeur in prose, however, did not end with Milton. Dryden did not wholly discard it, and Johnson added to it a statuesque massiveness while using it to more everyday purposes, and a homely morality and commonsense. At the beginning of my apprenticeship, however, I found both the verse and prose of Oliver Goldsmith more palatable to my youthful taste. With what ease and grace he moved within his phrases! Johnson was right in saying that 'he wrote like an angel'.

Johnson has been accused for being pompous in his prose style, and the glib critics have overlooked the vigour and clarity of his mind. No discussion of the skilful use of words, the manipulation of them (if I may be permitted this metaphor), can be better forwarded than by reference to Dr. Johnson's writings, especially his journalism in *The Idler* and *The Rambler* where he wrote essays of down-to-earth immediacy.

G. K. Chesterton was aware of this quality in the master whom, in character, he faintly resembled. A passage in his autobiography includes a mention of Johnson while explaining the advantages of the right placing of words, that practice with which I secondarily concerned myself while adding to my vocabulary, building passionately upon that habitual in a mildly literate family circle.

Chesterton is writing about the Yeats family, the gifted painters, father and son, and the second son, a poet of genius not, perhaps, fashionable in the decades after his death in 1939, but assured of immortality, on two counts—the quality of his poetry, and its seminal effect upon other poets. No matter how different in taste, in aesthetic principle, a poet may be, if he should turn in a period of sterility to Yeats's work, he will find himself eruptive again with creative impulse, and in his own idiom. Yeats does not make imitators of himself. He reawakens poets to their own unconscious selves, and their own practice in the placing of words.

Chesterton is so vividly pertinent on this matter of placing words. He says:

W. B. is perhaps the best talker I ever met, except his old father who alas will talk no more in this earthly tavern, though I hope he is still talking in Paradise. Among twenty other qualities, he had that rare but very real thing, entirely spontaneous style. The words will not come pouring out, any more than the bricks that make a great building come pouring out; they are simply arranged like lightning; as if a man could build a cathedral as quickly as a conjurer builds a house of cards. A long and elaborately balanced sentence, with dependent clauses alternative or antithetical, would flow out of such talkers with every word falling into its place, quite as immediately and innocently as most people would say it was a fine day or a funny business in the papers. I can still remember old Yeats, that graceful greybeard, saying in an offhand way about the South African War, 'Mr. Joseph Chamberlain has the character, as he has the face, of the shrewish woman who ruins her husband by her extravagance; and Lord Salisbury has the character, as he has the face, of the man who is so ruined.' That style, or swift construction of a complicated sentence, was the sign of a lucidity now largely lost. You will find it in the most spontaneous explosions of Dr. Johnson. Since then some muddled notion has arisen that talking in that complete style is artificial; merely because the man knows what he means and means to say it. I know not from what nonsense world the notion first came; that there is some connection between being sincere and being semi-articulate. But it seems to be a notion that a man must mean what he says, because he breaks down even in trying to say it, or that he must be a marvel of power and decision, because he discovers in the middle of a sentence that he does not know what he was going to say. Hence the conversation of current comedy.

That was written in 1936. Since then literary fashion, especially in the art of verse, has turned from incompetence to extravagant licence in the telescoping of images, inconsequential soliloquy, the mongering of slogans, and idle *non sequiturs*. This is due largely to the cult of deliberate subservience by the élite to the underdog, in a mood of guilt for the sins of their forefathers towards the humble workers in field and factory. Further, those workers, the mass of humanity, are no longer socially and economically humble, and are demanding, and getting, literary fodder to their taste, which is still tertiary. Bread and circuses, with lascivious variations, are generally precedent to an interest in arts based on a long, patient and disciplined growth in tradition, largely under aristocratic patronage.

This, to a critic of over-fastidious temperament, may account for the present state of the arts in Europe and America today. With the masses in the ascendency, able to command what they want, and to pay for it, a flood of primitive drum-beats, sexual in preference, has carried the younger generation away and the aesthetic disciplines with it, heaving and tossing under a banner labelled 'Experiment'.

Shakespeare put that experiment into the mouths of his yokels, clods and zanies whenever they interrupted the drama with their incoherent slapstick.

The real experiment, however, adding to the foundations of tradition, and thereby shoring up civilisation, is done by the craftsmen amongst the community, in the arts and every other creative activity. They are found in every grade of society, as also are the barbarians.

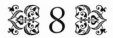

8

In this pursuit of the best arrangement of words, always under the spell of the music of language, I was, of course, drawn to the recognition of timing, marked by the comma, the semi-colon and the period, or full-stop.

There is never full agreement about this, and even after sixty years of practice, mostly professional, I find myself frequently uncertain of the right use of this small handful of tools, especially as between the semi-colon and the colon. This last decision is so much a matter of playing it by ear, to decide upon the necessary emphasis of the break between the clauses in question, and of the context within which they stand.

Even the comma has a looseness of usage, but I find, after years, decades of uncertainty, that it is best used if related to speech rhythm. That, I believe, is how Shakespeare (or his printers) used it in the dialogue of the plays. Certainly in verse, which I always write to be performed by the speaking voice, as music is composed to be performed by the singer or on instruments (which include the full orchestra as Berlioz used it), the comma coincides with a partial intake of breath at the top of the almost filled lungs, to give a pause that allows the emotional rhythm and the mental significance to make their simultaneous mark, upon reader and audience. In the right reading of verse, the reader should also be auditor, making that 'unheard music' which Keats said was sweeter than heard music.

Rhythm betrays the temperament of the artist. The most satisfying speaking of verse, or prose, is the result of a coincidence of the rhythms of the speaker and the writer, or if the speaker be an intelligent, trained interpreter, the subjection of his own natural rhythmic pulse to that of the writer.

The variations of rhythmic structure in writing are as infinite as the sum of the personalities and the themes involved. I suspect that it is a mathematical solecism to talk of the sum of two infinites; but the image suggests the vastness of the possibilities. Such odd quirks of habit, technique, physical and mental idiosyncrasy affect the result. The 'changes' in campanology are few by comparison.

An amusing example is offered by Montgomery Hyde in his book *Henry James at Home*. He says:

> Henry began the practice of dictating his stories about ten years previously, and by this time it was a confirmed habit from which he never departed. Its effects were easily recognisable in his style, which seemed to Theodora Bosanquet (his secretary) to become more and more like free, involved, unanswered talk. 'I know,' he once said to her, 'that I'm too diffuse when I'm dictating.' At the same time, he felt that the gain in expression through the use of what he laughingly called 'Remingtonese' more than compensated for any loss of concision. Indeed, at the time Theodora started her work for him, he had reached a stage at which, as she put it, the click of a Remington acted as a positive spur. According to her, he found it more difficult to compose to the music of any other make. 'During a fortnight when the Remington was out of order he dictated to an Oliver typewriter with evident discomfort, and he found it almost impossibly disconcerting to speak to something which made no responsive sound at all.' Once or twice when he was ill and in bed, Theodora would take down a note or two in shorthand, but as a rule he insisted on the Remington being moved into his bedroom even for the shortest letters.

That shows how easily a personal rhythm can be disturbed, or temporarily destroyed, like reflections in still water when a stone is thrown into a pond.

I remember an occasion years ago when a grandson demanded a 'long story' at a time when I was heavily committed with more professional contracts. I also had the service of a temporary secretary, an elderly woman who had no shorthand, and obviously no habit of taking a daily bath.

I proposed to dictate a story of about fifty thousand words, which she should tap out on the typewriter as I spoke them, with directions about punctuation and paragraphing.

We began, and so did my agony. The tale was to be about a group of five small boys exploring a cave. As I had, at that time, never been inside a cave, I must conjure out of the air not only the characters and behaviour of the young adventurers, but also the scene and its likely share in the drama.

The task had to be done in slow motion, for the un-fragrant typist was also un-expert. I found myself pacing the workroom, weaving both plot and paragraphs on the empty loom of air between me and the amanuensis, taking the occasions of the frequent broken threads of words as she laboriously wove them on the machine, to think ahead about my next adventures and phrases.

However, from time to time I unconsciously approached too near the table, and instantly the odour, like that stone in the pond, broke the imagined reflections, and dispelled the prose rhythm which was carrying them. I had to retreat to the other end of the workroom, and build up after a nerve-racking pause, the scene and movement so absurdly interrupted. This process went on for over a week, but the story was to be one of the most popular of any I have written. Maybe this is due to the effect of frustration, of thrusting against an intangible resistance, created by the hygienic and mechanical deficiencies of the typist. The consequent syncopation of the rhythm may have created just the right movement for the tale of the five boys groping underground towards an obscure crisis.

This example, with that of Henry James's addiction to the beat of the Remington typewriter, shows how elusive is this element of rhythm. Yet it is the foundation of all art, in whatever medium.

9

Like all other human intuition, it works with a seemingly simple mechanism, though a highly conscious artistry may be imposed on it by an intellectually and aesthetically skilled master.

I recall that when I was teaching myself how this mysterious union of inward urge and observant control was to be made, I studied a superb example of it in the prose of Thomas de Quincey. In the *English Opium Eater* there occurs a sentence which runs for nearly a page and a half: yet it pulses like the blood in our veins, firm and sure without a break, without a deviation, subservient to the need of the whole organism: all done by a perfect employment of punctuation, the full-stop being held in suspense by a series of nicely graded clauses, their surprise regulated by colon and semi-colon, so that the reader's attention never flags, indeed is commanded, until the period is dropped like a final drum-tap. Garrulity was never put to better use, nor a drug-bemused imagination so efficiently directed.

Technical skill of this kind, which also deliberates the placing and movement of words, is to be cultivated as a duty by every writer. It is an exercise that benefits both writer and reader, for it tends towards clear and immediate presentation of meaning.

A simple, harsh punctuation is the first rule in journalism, especially in the tabloid press. The majority of readers of newspapers want information, and they want it quickly and briefly. The short sentence without a qualifying clause, is the vehicle for this: and the sentence must have a punch in it. The selected information must be hurled at the reader. This device is said to make the selection of facts more convincing. It is a partial approach to the shouting of slogans that sway mobs during riots. The full-stop after the single statement comes down like a grenade. The sentences tramping down the columns of the *Daily Rouser* offer no pause for individual thought, especially second thought. Second thought usually requires an auxiliary clause, in qualification. That leads to complexity, to some degree of sophistication of mind, and nerves, which welcomes the use of a colon, a semi-colon, a comma, with the significance of their various timing.

This matter of *tempo* is most interesting because it is connected so revealingly with the variations and changes of social habit. There is a world-wide complaint that everything in life is being speeded up. Maybe this was always so. The complaint may have a physiological origin, away back in the primitive conditions of life amongst the cave-dwellers of the last ice-age. Their bodily and mental equipment just could not cope with the rush of events. Since the dawn of literacy, records have remarked on this neurosis, and have symbolised it as God- or Devil-imposed affliction. The main purpose of the New Testament has been to establish the authority of a doctor to cure it. Peace, patience, serenity, 'making haste slowly', these are the medicines against the attacks, unremitting and furious, of the *Eumenides*.

Since the invention of power-driven machinery, this urge towards an ever faster way of life has risen like a gathering hurricane. Nearly a century ago, Samuel Butler predicted in his book *Erewon*, that inevitably a crisis would come in which either man or the machine must be master. Today, we may suspect that the crisis has passed, and that the machine has won. Human muscles, human nerves, human spirits, are enslaved to the machine and its mania for speed.

This is a vast proposition, with infinite ramifications for argument, for and against. But here I am concerned with the effect of this racial neurosis on our languages, our patterns of words. Not only the popular newspapers reflect it, with their machine-gun prose. Parliamentary debate, academic lecturing, narrative in the writing of history, fiction, biography; metrical structures in verse, with the placing of imagery and rhyme, all are affected in the same way. All are swept along like fallen leaves before a gale.

The change in our use and arrangement of words can be seen by comparing the prose pattern of extracts 'from our columns twenty-five years ago' given by many of our daily newspapers. The prose was more formal, ornamental, almost pompous. It is comparable in its present content to a square of flowered wall-paper stuck on a plain distempered wall in a modern utility house. It is a period piece, after only twenty-five years.

What will be the influence of a mechanically driven society after another quarter of a century? The speed increases almost by geometrical progression. Maybe we shall have done with language altogether, impatient with the laborious, clumsy, hand-wrought craft of fitting words together. The symbols of the mathematician, and the physicist, propelled instantly by instruments such as the television screen and the computer, will have become a common means of human communication. I remember that some thirty years ago Compton Mackenzie predicted to me that by the end of the century, books would no longer be a normal vehicle of cultural life, either for practical or aesthetic purposes. He said the profession of letters would be finished. I noted the gleam of mischief in that eloquent eye, and I know what passionate concern lodged in the mind illuminating it; the mind of a master in the art whose extinction he was so ironically foretelling. I writhed and protested, but he repeated his comic prophecy, increasing the mischievous gleam, so that the eye became baleful.

Since then, the symbols of the scientists have spread their technical control into outer space. They have stamped the prints of four pairs of gumboots on the vitreous dust of the moon's surface, and recorded a close-up of the icy cap of our neighbouring planet over a distance of sixty million miles.

What have words done to compare with that? They have been our medium probably for several hundreds of thousands of years, yet most of us use only a handful of them, and with the utmost diffidence and uncertainty. Is the medium of language basically primitive, like the ideologies, the superstitions, the myths it has created, destroyed and embalmed, during the evolution of the human race?

We appear to be cutting the medium down to size, pruning it of the ornaments and convolutions of rhetoric, poetic image and metaphor. We use it now in a sort of telegraphic compression, and package it in cliché and slogan-wrapping, for quicker and more democratic transmission to the newly and semi-literate masses of an ever-increasing population. But even so it does not convey our needs and our sophistications fast enough. Speed is still our dominant preoccupation, in physical transport from one place to another, as also in our mental unrest.

Was the playful prophecy of a masterly professional writer, thirty years ago, more ominous than he intended? Is it already being proven by what is happening today, in what is called 'the Space Age'? In the pattern of the future evolution of man, is there no indication that the weaving of word-shapes into literary form will be needed, or even tolerated? The scientists have already substituted synthetic materials, to replace less reliable metals and natural drugs. Will words also be relegated with those more tangible elements, and the poet lose his vocation, with the medicine-man and the priest?

PART FOUR

Living the words

1

What is the answer to that volley of pessimistic questions, which I have so solemnly, funereally, deduced from Sir Compton Mackenzie's provocative suggestion made when human society was comparatively static, only thirty years ago?

I believe that in trying to find an answer I shall have to evoke the ghosts of beliefs and acceptances already buried by a great many people in this 'Space Age' society. For the scientific achievement which has fastened this label on our way of life has brought instantaneous changes into our general conceptions of the mystery of the universe. And with those changes, our faith has also suffered a space-change.

The proving by Copernicus and Galileo that the Earth is round, and is not the centre of the sidereal system, had a like effect, on every aspect of human consciousness; its religious forms, its philosophies, its aesthetics.

But we look back now, over the perspective of the centuries, and see that the confusion, the violent revolution four centuries ago in thought and political actions, in the arts and crafts, was not wholly destructive. We see that it was a release, and an opportunity for expansion. We even called it *The Renaissance*. We see too that it also turned to rediscovery, putting new and wider interpretations upon many of the techniques and theories of the culture whose principal tenet that the earth was flat had proved to be false.

The influence of men of genius, however, always creates a momentary vacuum. The word *influence* means an incoming, a flood, and such a dynamic change draws instantly a rush of formerly static flotsam to fill the gap. That flotsam is the body of followers of the genius, the cashers-in, the exploiters, the didacts and theorists, who hasten to settle a new dogma, which they can fashion into an academy where they can resume administration.

There must always be an institution. We see it being reimposed, and with such dreadful emphasis and redoubled intolerance, in the new political structures of the human race in the twentieth century.

This reaction has been so swift, and on so vast a scale, that it has started up a chain reaction of further and fragmented revolutions. The arts are reflecting this social welter, and there is more opportunity than ever before, to encourage chicanery and untrained incompetence in the practice of the arts, and pompous pseudo-theorising about the fraudulent results.

These sudden breaks with tradition are no new thing however. Between the two world wars the late Rose Macaulay wrote a novel called *They were Defeated*. One of the principal characters in it is a figure from life and literature, the poet Robert Herrick, who flourished (the word is most appropriate to his verse) through a period of violent changes in the society around him. Born in 1591, the son of a prosperous London goldsmith, he led a gay Cavalier life after his terms at Cambridge, but the economic disturbances of the Civil War forced him to seek a profession in addition to dalliance with 'women, wine and song'.

He chose the Church, and retreated to a rustic living in Devon, where he contrived to be an adequate parson without wholly relinquishing the dalliance. Indeed, the flirtation with 'song' became a marriage, and it produced a body of lyric poetry which is immortal. Some of it is devotional, but the majority is pagan, epicurean, almost oriental in its exquisite precision and point. His tiny themes, some of which could be inscribed on a cherry stone, are comparable to the epigrams written in pre-Christian ages by Chinese scholars languishing as Civil Service officials in some remote province of that mainly bucolic Empire.

In similar circumstances Herrick amused himself. Bored or unwell, he used that experience thus:

> Then make me weep
> My pains asleep;

And give me such reposes
That I, poor I,
May think thereby
I live and die
'Mongst roses.

Rose Macaulay lifts this character, incongruous contemporary of the majestic Milton, and poses him, in his later life, within his decision to revisit Cambridge, urged by a desire for some more intelligent appreciation of his poetry than his parishioners were capable of.

He had not reckoned for the change of fashion in verse-making, consequent upon the neo-platonist revival of religious fervour, the Anglicanism re-acting after the Restoration, from the purgative puritanism of the so-called Commonwealth. The reaction took the form of an elaborate cult of metaphysical philosophy. Many good poets became spokesmen of this religious movement, and their work survives today. But at the time, the most famous was Abraham Cowley, and his inflated reputation was due to the fact that he carried the new cult, and the involved expression of it, to excess.

Rose Macaulay, learned in the history of that phase of Anglicanism, and therefore nicely particular and vivid in her presentation of the scene when the old Anacreontic Herrick came back to Cambridge, expectant of fame, has drawn a tragi-comic picture of what happened. Herrick was totally ignored, and he was so chagrined that he went home and died of obscurity, as well as old age, in 1674.

I

2

Literary history is repeating itself today, reflecting former social upheavals. The speed of the changes in fashion is greater. As long ago as the 1920s the poet Ralph Hodgson (his output of verse small but permanent) said to me that a poetic generation then was about five years. He was referring to Keats's doleful apostrophe to the nightingale that 'no hungry generations tread thee down'.

Nowadays, the poetic generations tread on each other's heels month by month, and the ageing practitioner is at a loss to number them. By the time he first hears of a new young master poet, that master is already two ranks ahead on the way to banishment.

I find, therefore, that the poets who were my immediate predecessors, along with the composers and painters, their contemporaries, are now bundled off under the label 'Georgian', occasionally and dismissively referred to as 'suburban rustic' tweed-clad escapists. They are thought to be so remote that by this diminishment one cannot be distinguished from another.

Of my own generation, which succeeded them, the dismissal is not so absolute because it contained the pioneers of the technical explorations in all directions, many of them ending in the desert where 'no bird sings', and intelligibility is lost, as well as the melodic line.

I see little aesthetic coherence in the work of my own generation, the 'lost generation' decimated during the 1914–1918 war. Some of them died singing, notably Edward Thomas and Wilfred Owen. There were many other victims who made a valuable contribution to that sacrificial music, but the poetry of these two is accepted by the young critics fifty years later.

Three of that generation survived the war, and continued to write verse, and prose, submissive to the traditional discipline of the craft, and showing no selfconscious concern to startle their readers by new verbal devices that might bring the writers a quick notoriety. Siegfried Sassoon, Edmund Blunden, Robert Graves, like their elders, Hardy, Yeats and De La Mare, have all used words without consciously striving after self-advertisement by means of some distortion in the choice and placing of them. They have been content with grammar, and humbly laboured to make their verbal structures firmly set on recognisable foundations. But could any group of writers be more distinctively individual than these who, in the mysterious values which I am trying to disclose in this essay, are wholly successful, each through his own undeliberated originality?

I do not imply that they lack experiment in their art. Thomas Hardy, for example, writing a poem about the age-old theme of a girl waiting in vain for her lover, shows the passing of time, and loads it with disappointment by using a blockage of syllables to describe the sound of the church clock. There the girl stood alone 'while the tryst-hour stroked its sum'. The reader at once is made aware of some element in the choice of words that reveals the character, the personality of the writer, without his conscious effort to do so. It also adds to the tradition of verbal usage without abusing it. Finally, it carries an overtone, not only of the sound of the bell, but that unaccountable presence of something additional to meaning; a light, a revelation, that nourishes our consciousness as does personal experience. It is unforgettable because it is truly poetry, oracular, the work of a 'maker', as poets were called when this power, this authority, was fully ascribed to them by a devout and credulous community.

But the recognisable presence of that power in words which has a physical effect, like wind, rain or sunshine, on the reader's whole person, can show itself in more everyday, ordinary words, set in a more ordinary sequence, than those by Hardy which I have quoted.

Roy Campbell, a rumbustious poet who was savagely rejected by his contemporaries in the 1930s because of his unfashionable political views, wasted much of his time and

talent attacking his critics with satirical verse, whose edge has
now rusted. But in his rich, rhetorical poems, Parnassian in
grandeur, like the work of 'Victor Hugo, Alas!', there shines
again and again this pure light of the pure essence, which we
see, hear, smell so often in nature, so rarely in the arts. In his
famous anthology piece, 'Horses on the Camargue', there are
four lines which refer to rough weather across that saline
landscape:

> But when the great gusts rise
> And lash their anger on these arid coasts,
> When the scared gulls career with mournful cries
> And whirl across the wastes like driven ghosts . . .

The directness and simplicity in those last two lines lift the
verse into the elements with the seabirds whose erratic flight it
describes, and the reader feels that nervous disturbance in the
solar plexus, the reaction which A. E. Housman required as a
catalyst for depositing the gold of poetry out of the dilutions of
literature.

The encounter is something in real life, or at least a parallel to
it. In a poem on 'The Spell of France', Edmund Blunden begins:

> Little enough of that wide country,
> Though fascinated long,
> Have I as yet acquired; that little
> Is constant undersong,
> Astonishment, rest, recognition,
> In my life's round;
> And whether I will or no my silence
> Reverts to that bright ground.

This vital force of beauty within the words, which I am trying
to find with only intermittent success, as though it were the
ever-retreating voice of Delius's 'first cuckoo in spring', pulses
through that opening stanza of Blunden's declaration of love
for the country where he fought in the blood-soaked mud of the

trenches in 1914–18, an experience that added a new dimension to the character of his youthful bucolic verse; one of anger, despair, suspicion and irony. But the magic light was not quenched. It shines through his old-fashioned technique, that still uses inversions such as 'Though fascinated long', as idiosyncratic and un-modish as Hardy's quaint, obsolete syntax.

These practices are impatiently rejected by the latter-day critics in the second half of the twentieth century, though latter-day puritans, they eagerly accept new artifices which more abruptly disrupt the melodic line, the 'constant undersong' that Blunden, Sassoon and Graves have brought again and again to the reader's hearing in their lifelong practice of the art.

3

It is heard not only in the work of widely experienced and recognised poets. It is independent of fame and immortality. I found it, for example, while writing this essay, in a collection of newly published poems by the North Country poet Phoebe Hesketh. In a short verse of ten lines called 'The Heron', the evocation ends:

> Movement without sound; the evening drifts
> On autumn tides of colour, light, and smell
> Of warm decay; and now the heron lifts
> Enormous wings in elegy; a grey
> Shadow that seems to bear the light away.

There, too, the 'movement without sound', like Blunden's 'constant undersong', the magic spell works, and poetry is apparent, not through technical perfection, nor by new devices and rejecting of traditional forms. The last line of that conjuration of atmosphere might have been even more effective without the reservation, the touch of dubiety, if it were shortened to

> Shadow that bears the light away.

the line, truncated by one foot, increasing the sensation of loneliness, and the night closing over the scene.

These poets whom I have named, and the quotations, represent the carrying of traditional verse forms and phraseology into our own time. They stand now like megaliths alongside a motorway, or a holiday camp. The modern way of life, mechanised, overcrowded, rootless and raucous, invades and destroys the natural landscape, whose beauty and quietude it seeks as authentic. The process is an immediate product of the prosperity given by the democratic freedoms and releases. It is not new. It is only an uncontrolled, probably uncontrollable enlargement of human conduct through the ages, which in the main tends towards barbaric wreckage and filth, indifference to historical values, and horrifying cruelty and injustice to individuals by society in the name of some religious or political ideology, through an incompetent and clumsy bureaucratic machine.

In saying this, I am not wandering from my central theme; nor am I indulging a bias against the inevitable consequences of the sudden proliferation of the human race, and the contradictory needs which this necessitates. Maybe, in the distant future, an earthly paradise may be evolved out of the increasing efforts to run affairs with just the right balance between reason and emotion; science and politics.

But the twentieth century is not likely to be seen by future historians as much different from the millennia preceding it back into pre-history, except in the speed of its development.

Meanwhile, the arts reflecting it are equally violent, equally contradictory, especially in their formal structures. So are the critics discussing those arts. In general, they are partisan of the iconoclasts; they welcome the extremes of eccentric experiment, and they dismiss as irrelevant all work rooted in tradition, or touched by that quietism which is anathema today, as a relic of spiritual and intellectual aloofness.

Because of these highly strung symptoms of the feverish and nomadic articulations of modern life, there is the inevitable reaction amongst the minority who look back with appreciation to the habits of west European society which were broken by the two world wars and the tyranny of the machine and electronics. The tyranny is that of triumph, the drug of success. It has given mankind powers which only half a century ago he ascribed solely to God, the Creator whom he now largely repudiates, or at least puts under temporary arrest as a philosophic malingerer.

The discomforts of this way of life begin to outweigh the advantages. Its theory, called existentialism, is equally prone to disaster, and so are the arts based on that *ad hoc* philosophy which is no novelty, but only a speeded up (everything today having to be given an element of extravaganza to match our racial high temperature) fragment of Epicureanism.

This theory, with the circumstances of our environment, the *olla podrida* of cultures stirred together by modern transport, that devilish dynamic, we see reflected in the turmoil of the arts.

The first signs of the breakdown were not disruptive. Bergson, Santayana, Croce, by their exploration of aesthetics, offered a benevolent and devout control of the breakaway from realism and the objective representation of nature. They gave direction to the analysis of intuition and subjective outlook introduced by the impressionist painters, and the symbolist poets, whose practice in France immediately reawakened the imaginations of artists throughout the Western world.

The American Ezra Pound, and his friend and disciple T. S. Eliot, whose work the older man publicised, brought the experimental and ultimately disruptive practices into English writing round about the beginning of the second decade of the century, challenging the poets whom they wrongly dismissed as a homogeneous group, 'the Georgians', merely because their work appeared in the anthologies collected by the conservative connoisseur, Edward Marsh.

Those poets are still under a cloud today. It hides their differences as well as their valuable qualities. Lascelles Abercrombie, Gordon Bottomley, John Freeman, John Drinkwater and many others, can be rediscovered individually, and their poetry panned for the grains of gold.

It will be seen that they too were searching for fresh air, after the patchouli and affectations of the *fin de siècle* poets of the 1890s: though even those decadents are not to be wholly dismissed. The moment of miracle occurs even in unpropitious times. The experience of that moment is implied in the repeated line of a rondel written by one of those poets, Arthur Symons, who at the turn of the century was an influential critic. He introduced the work of the French *Symbolistes* to English readers, and thus pointed the way of technical revolution to Pound and

Eliot. The line I have in mind is haunting in its context. It may not unfairly be quoted with reference to that touch of verbal magic which the more pedestrian critic George Saintsbury called 'the poetic moment, the sudden transcendence and transfiguration which sits upon a phrase or idea'. The recurring line in Arthur Symons's pretty little artifice is 'All things vanish, you remain'.

4

We have still to discover what it is, in the use of words, that vanishes, and what it is that remains. Ezra Pound and Eliot, following such French innovators and rebels as Mallarmé, Jules Laforgue, and Rimbaud, attacked both by theory and practice the whole structure of literary tradition in English. The campaign was complicated, however, by their conservative attitude in historical and religious matters. Reacting against the pioneering crudeness of society in the United States, their native land, they were attracted towards medieval thought and its concise disciplines. So esoteric imagery out of the scholastic past, both of Europe and the Orient, was presented by them in the colloquial terminology of our contemporary English and American city life.

Through the dialogue in Eliot's poem *Sweeney Agonistes*, the problems of this self-contradictory impulse are revealed to the reader whose taste is habituated to a hieratic gesture in the poetic use of words. Eliot called the poem 'fragments of an Aristophanic melodrama', thus further emphasising the deference to literary precedent in the title of the poem, where he doffs his cap to Milton, the word-master whose technique he attacked with vigour in his early essays in criticism, the opening of the campaign.

The challenge in that campaign, and the poems to justify it, found followers among the younger generation after the social upheaval following the First World War. The shock of genocidal violence still maddened mankind. It deprived the Versailles Conference of wisdom and held Western civilisation in a state of delirium. Europeans and Americans danced to the beat of tropical drums.

Eliot's and Pound's verse caught that rhythm. *Sweeney Agonistes* voiced the distraught nervous mood of the post-war world. Sweeney cried out, symbolising the recent horrors that

I knew a man once did a girl in
Any man might do a girl in
Any man has to, needs to, wants to
Once in a lifetime, do a girl in.

He lifted the facts of a contemporary crime case from the newspapers and gave them a universal reference, but in verse that rejected the pre-war concepts of poetic temper; the melodic line that secures the serenity which is the essence of a fully authoritative and permanent work of art, wrought from 'emotion remembered in tranquillity'; Wordsworth's definition and practice.

What is so paradoxical is that Eliot should have been the man to establish and popularise the rejection of these age-old aesthetic acceptances, rooted in history, religion, myth, folklore.

He was in temperament no democrat, no likely spokesman of revolt, no glib rabble-rouser. He was such an un-American American that he became a naturalised Englishman, immediately retreating still further into Anglicanism, the last refuge of our insular preservationists; social, political and literary. The Jacobean Prayer Book, with its poised and fastidious choice of words, so profoundly loaded, so grave in pace, is an extreme remove from the innovations which Eliot brought from America, via Paris, into English verse. Echoes of Walt Whitman's resonant catalogues, Jules Laforgue's distracted street-walkings, and Ezra Pound's staccato exclamatory *non sequiturs*, ring through the broken rhythms by which Eliot tried to voice the bewilderment with which mankind stared at the consequences of its recent, world-wide attack of insanity, which had more than 'done a girl in'. It had done a civilisation in.

But still, as Eliot made Sweeney cry out:

I've gotta use words when I talk to you,
But here's what I was going to say.

> He didn't know if he was alive
> and the girl was dead
> He didn't know if the girl was alive
> and he was dead
> He didn't know if they were both alive
> or both were dead.

This epoch-breaking poet was aware of his predicament. His temperament had driven him from middle-west America to Europe, hungry for scholastic food, the preservations of the cultural past, of intellectual aristocracy, and the fastidious refinements of literatures rooted two thousand years deep and still articulate in Europe's spoken languages.

This conflict of temperament with revolutionary purpose in the literary field, may account for Eliot's nervous, often sardonic manner in his social life. It made him cautious, self-critical. He admonished himself while he criticised the persistent use of pre-war poetic techniques. And he did so by using those long, melodic cadences, and even the images, which Milton and Wordsworth had stabilised in our prosody. He rebukes himself:

> Do not suddenly break the branch, or
> Hope to find
> The white hart behind the white well,
> Glance aside, not for lance, do not spell
> Old enchantments. Let them sleep.
>   'Gently dip, but not too deep',
> Lift your eyes
> Where the roads dip and where the roads rise
> Seek only there
> Where the grey light meets the green air
> The hermit's chapel, the pilgrim's prayer.

We see, or rather hear, how the impersonal and absolute authority of pure poetry soars above Eliot's other purposes;

ethical, missionary, personally ambitious to make a mark in a field already trampled and overcrowded.

Yet he will not accept that authority. 'Old enchantments. Let them sleep', he cries.

5

This was the complicated character of the man whom I first met in the January of 1921, and with him, Herbert Read, who was his ally in the proposal to find a new literary form that would carry the wreckage of the war-shattered world as material towards a new site and a new cultural structure.

I have described in a book *The Voyage Home*, the third volume of an essay in autobiography, how in that year when Europe was still in a condition of post-operative shock after the war, a group of young writers drew together for weekly meetings, first for evening meals in an upper room of a little Italian restaurant called the Commercio in Soho, opposite the house where Hazlitt lived. After a year or two, we met for luncheons in another room over a public house in Beauchamp Place, Knightsbridge. The change was made because Herbert Read, who had been Private Secretary to the head of the Civil Service in the office of the Treasury, got himself transferred to the Victoria and Albert Museum, in order to have more congenial official work, and more freedom to further his interest in literature and the plastic arts.

So we all suited ourselves to his locality. That was taken for granted, without question. The acceptance showed our respect, and increasing affection, for this silent Yorkshire dalesman, bony of feature, reserved and granitic in manner. He was, I think, closer to Eliot in friendship than any of us. Both were enigmatic: and an enigma is always attractive, especially to more volatile bodies, such as the Imagiste poet, F. S. Flint, a fiery particle of great height surmounted by a cloud of flaming hair blown about by the emotional storms of the brain below.

We all, at that time, earned our living by other than literary work. Read, Flint and I were civil servants, Alec Randall in the Foreign Service, Eliot in Lloyds Bank.

Round that nucleus of five there fluttered several associates, one of whom, an ex-professional soldier named Bonamy Dobrée, was to have a successful career in the academic world. His was a valuable contribution to the group, for he was both gentle and incisive. He did much to induce the university faculties of English to admit the innovations so relentlessly urged by Eliot and Read.

The vehicle for our activities was the quarterly magazine, *The Criterion*, edited by Eliot and financed by Lady Rothermere. It tried to cover the whole of European literary life, printing contributions from foreign writers, and reviewing their books. F. S. Flint covered the French field, J. B. Trend the Spanish, and Alec Randall the German. Occasional contributors handled books in other languages.

Outside my friendship with Eliot and Read, which grew like a tree with the years, decade by decade, my acceptance of their theories and their creative work was reluctant. I found the theories too cerebral, too aesthetically puritanical and restrictive. They deliberately pruned the fruit-bearing branches of their imaginations to fit the shape of the theories. At that time they were merciless towards the past, and they dismissed traditional forms.

I remember being angry one day when Eliot said to me that he could no longer read sonnets. The form was dead for him.

On another occasion, at a luncheon where he had brought the classical scholar Lowes Dickinson as his guest, at the time of the publication of *The Waste Land*, I spoke to Eliot about his cryptic imagery and he replied by saying that he feared the poem was too long and diffuse. I thought this was a perverse remark, hardly sincere. It closed our discussion, but with no acrimony.

Both he and Read knew that I could not share their evangelism for the new art; the esoteric and subjective explorations of the whims, resentments, social bitterness disguised in a pretence of detached presentation of the mundane scene with its mechanical novelties, its vulgarity and garish commercial display.

Their precept and practice have won through, to conquer

world-wide the arts today. What they advocated has become established. Both have been honoured and lavishly decorated, and to the days of their death, they remained unpoisoned by fame. Indeed, age brought them out of the hardness of their pioneering years, and gave them a geniality which made contact with them the more endearing.

But I look at the side-issues of their influence, and my youthful wariness has become dismay. I see how their advocacy of experiment in formal novelty has given the charlatan, the shirker from self-discipline, and the commercial cheapjack, *carte blanche* certificates of acceptance, before the mildly credulous public, and also in the academies and galleries.

All manner of fraudulent fancy, with no form, no articulation, no craftsmanship, is offered as creative art, in music, sculpture, painting, and literature, and is solemnly, pedantically discussed in the press and technical magazines, in terms no more intelligible than the rubbish so crookedly scrutinised. These are indeed the days of 'The Emperor's Shirt'.

This imposition flourishes upon the social tendencies of our time, which are still whirling in disruption after the break-up caused by the sudden impact of so many contributory factors, the wars, the new technologies, the effect of psychological analysis upon the taboos of religious dogmas, the urbanisation of rural life, the whole gamut of exploratory and intrusive science. It is wearisome to try to enumerate the 'slings and arrows of outrageous fortune' which are still converging upon the bleeding body politic of mankind.

6

During the intellectual and moral turmoil of those formative years, when as a writer I gradually settled down from naive amateurism to a full-time professional vocation, I still battled alone towards my concept of the best use of words: best personally, socially, aesthetically.

Only F. S. Flint stayed on in the Ministry of Labour, which I left to become editor of the publishing firm who had produced several of my books in verse and in prose. Herbert Read and T. S. Eliot had already preceded me in this change from amateur to professional status. Read took the Chair of Fine Arts at Edinburgh University, and an editorial post at Routledges. Eliot left Lloyds Bank to become editor in what was at that time Faber and Gwyer, with the scholarly poet Geoffrey Faber as his co-operative chairman. Thus the three of us were in positions to be able to encourage young poets, by backing our fancy in publishing work we believed to carry gold of sufficient purity.

Our triple contribution to the bibliographical history of the years between the wars and through the Second World War into the nineteen-fifties, is a matter outside the scope of this present essay on the mystery of the usage of words. We all backed some winners, whose success from the publisher's point of view carried the rest of the series which we sponsored.

Shop-talk, however, interests only the shopkeepers. A publisher's editor has to secure the agreement of his directors, who foot the bills; and that is always an incalculable relationship, in taste, responsibility, and point of view. When one of us wanted to publish a book of verse and could not persuade his directors to accept the venture, he would sometimes pass on the rejected poet to one or other of the trio. That practice produced some trade secrets which shall remain unrevealed.

It would be interesting to learn how far our work as book-sieves for publishers influenced our own writings. The occupa-

K

tion, no unusual one in the world of letters, involves the reading of hundreds of manuscripts, and a glance at many hundreds more whose opening paragraphs reveal that further exploration is unnecessary. It is a task which can induce staleness of mind, such as Solomon felt when he sighed 'of the making of books there is no end'. It is also rather a mortuary occupation, for the percentage of still births after literary orgasms is well over ninety-nine.

I remember that at our weekly luncheons, we often looked at each other with dreadful, silent enquiry. Sometimes we even discussed our fear of the disease which threatens all professional people; the inertia and loss of enthusiasm due to being confronted by so much well-meant but worthless verbiage.

I suspect that George Meredith was suffering from that illness, when, as reader for Constable's, he rejected Thomas Hardy's first novel. That was no isolated mistake. There are also other dangers. Creative artists, and no doubt creative folk in all other walks of life, are frequently the slaves of their own demon. The urge that causes them to be exceptional in vitality often canalises all their powers, intellectual, spiritual, even physical, and prevents them from appreciating the same mysterious force at work in other individuals, but by different idioms.

The creative mind lives with fear, because it is entertaining a stranger whom it cannot fully trust or understand. It is thus open to jealousy, prejudice, and all the other symptoms of self-protectiveness.

These morbid conditions breed freely in persons too deeply involved in the day to day working of their professions. Writers cannot escape. They are indeed notorious, because by reason of the nature of their gifts and expertise, they are expressive, and widely expressive, of their feelings. So the public hears too much about them.

I endured these dangers for twenty years, as a publisher's adviser, but by comparison with the preceding twenty-four years as a civil servant, the experience was paradisal. I was at last principally concerned with words, the force which had picked me out in my boyhood and made me that special kind of monomaniac.

No man is more fortunate than he who earns his living by a craft which consumes him, demands all his attention and skill, sums up for him the whole worth and significance of his life on earth. One can become romantic and rhapsodic on this matter, and frowned upon, especially by fellow professionals, whether one be a poet or a cabinet maker, a doctor or a priest. But in medieval times, all crafts, all professions, were rightly called 'mysteries', and it is in this sense that I write of my almost lifelong preoccupation with words. It is an approach to craftsmanship which the old guilds proclaimed.

It lingers on even into the twentieth century, the age of mass-production and mechanical division of labour. It voiced itself one day when I was at work in my study, while a builder's man was fitting a slow-combustion stove. When the job was done, he turned to me and said, 'Now, sir, would you like me to explain the *philosophy* of the stove?'

I accepted the offer with double gratitude. For the same reason, or supra-reason, I accepted the offer of those twenty years of close scrutiny of other people's efforts in literary inflammation, picking out here and there what I believed to be an achievement of the authentic, clear flame, the light of the Word.

7

These asides of shop-talk, are meant to show the soil in which the seedling grew; how it was jostled and shadowed by similar implantations in other obsessionists; and finally, how the hardening processes of the change from youthful amateur excitement to steady, methodical professional purpose did not wither it at the root.

My editorial work made me alert to the infinite variety of the ways in which people use words. Thirty years ago, the manuscripts submitted were recognisably imitative; an acceptable sign of the humble beginner. Latterday permissiveness in life has changed that gambit. Eccentricity and exhibitionism have ousted patient apprenticeship. Robert Louis Stevenson said that he 'played the sedulous ape' to the masters whose writing seemed to him to be excellent. Today, much of the material offered for publication shows little sign of being sedulous, and much of being simian rather than human, especially if it claims to be in verse.

That difference, however, raises the question of the change of cultural epochs, and the possible growth of new standards in art, anti-pathetic to a veteran. This question has gone down the ages, and still remains unanswerable.

But personal experience, and long practice, are always valuable, as a fulcrum on which to balance the scales of judgment, in every human activity. I have, therefore, dismissed my hesitation about introducing some shop-talk into this study of the use of words. It is a roundabout means of levering my way into the heart of the matter.

The remark, for instance, by Eliot that he feared he had not sufficiently pared down the verse in *The Waste Land* has haunted my mind persistently. At the time I suspected it as a riposte against my reserved attitude towards his poetry. But the years passed; I got to know him better, and the subtle sincerity of his complex character.

The incident is now recalled more understandingly. It continues to make me cautious when confronted with writing that is strange to my ear, and an affront to my sense of aesthetic values, founded in my own instincts and tested through a lifetime of work in the field of letters, reading and writing, the steady systole and diastole which regulate the impulses of life, and command its rhythm.

The remarkable thing is, that by broadening in this way my acceptance of the variety in other writers' work, I have found it to be a reciprocal discipline in cultivating my own. The process is not altogether a conscious one; I notice it only intermittently. No doubt it is comparable to the effect on people of their maturing in social contacts, learning to be tolerant and courteous, and to reduce, or at least disguise, natural tendencies to be dogmatic and aggressive.

Thus I imply a moral factor in this matter of aesthetics, which shows 'art for art's sake' to be perpetually incomplete, though it comes so conspicuously into any discussion or study of any art, as a craft with technical requirements.

The compelling and persuasive use of words demands an open-minded and nervous awareness of those requirements. How that awareness is turned to assurance can only be shown by example. It cannot be taught. It can only be learned, and I am not sure that it can be learned by conscious effort. That is where the moral factor enters.

This statement is likely to be repudiated with contempt by most contemporary critics and the practitioners whom they acclaim. They have thrown out the concept of the moral impulse in art, and put in its place the political, the social inducement. The indignation of economics, with a secular credo, provides the poetic heat, and it has burned away from the Pauline reminder of 'faith, hope and *caritas*' the last, most mysterious and powerful of the three armaments, that of love.

But love is the universal fecundity. It is the mother of morals. My lifelong experience and practice as a writer has convinced me that love is also the mother of the arts, indeed of all things made through creative skill by man. The belief goes even further, to the environment in which man exists, the material forms of earth, with its flora and fauna, the infinity of other substantial bodies, is spaceless space and timeless time; through all that to the new partially comprehended intermission between energy, or idea, and its deposit, the atom.

Man, by his sciences, has tapped at the outposts of that ultimate mystery, and appears to be in danger of destroying himself by reaching even thus far.

But during this epoch of triumphant advance in physical knowledge, he has allowed his philosophic and aesthetic specu-lation to turn against the concept of worship, and to strip from the word 'love' its symbolism of that primal creative force from which his science has stolen an iota of its secret.

Thus, my claim that the use of words as an art is an act of worship, a gesture of love, an assertion of faith and hope, even in its negative outcry against those distinctions, in the face of suffering and defeat, will cause my essay to be dismissed as a survival of the now detested romanticism which fuelled the creative fires of nineteenth-century man. I shall be called a hypocrite. I shall be reminded of the historical superficiality of my statement, because it ignores the horrors of economic and social injustice and unequality of those times, no different from the evils which have persisted throughout our human story.

I can reply that destructiveness, cynicism, obsession with material problems, either through legislation or revolution, science or philosophy, have no relevance to the simplicity of love, the first-and-last force which Dante, more than any other artist, came near to revealing in the last lines of his *Divine Comedy*, seven hundred years ago, in a vision based on a faith in unity, a concept which our scientists are carrying into the laboratory today, with dire temerity.

Meanwhile, in our arts, we are rejecting this drawing together of knowledge towards a consciousness of interrelated unity. Our artists are concerned with subjective exclamation through snatches of borrowed media; the sexual drum-beat of African and American tribal rituals; scraps of shattered machinery from our own factory products. It is as though they are concerned only with a fragmented despair, the slums of a broken culture, looking in the direction pointed out by Eliot in the nervous frenzy of his early poems, through which he foretold a crisis of Western civilisation,

> Aware of the damp souls of housemaids
> Sprouting despondently at area gates

and saw in that symbol

> The last twist of the knife.

8

Yet the structure of human society, and the problems of justice and suffering, were never less oppressive than they are today. It is not solely from these matters of material environment that words draw their mysterious vitality.

The tumid growth of industrial urbanism, and the festive wanderings of its vast populations released from poverty, have made poetic references to the countryside obsolete. But what was the actuality of that countryside in the past? Man has always been untidy; a maker of middens. No doubt Edward Fairfax accepted them as a necessary ingredient of human environment when he sat, translating Tasso's *Gerusalemme Liberta* in 1604, in the Golden but insanitary Age of England's verbal glory. But he also wrote, without a thought of satire or irony,

> Now from the fresh, the soft, and tender bed,
> Of her still mother gentle night out-flew,
> The fleeting balme on hilles and dales shee shed,
> With honey drops of pure and precious dew,
> And on the verdure of greene forrests spred,
> The virgin prime-rose, and the violet blew,
> And sweet-breathed Zephire on his spreading wings
> Sleepe, ease, repose, rest, peace and quiet brings.

That verse, especially its last line, is a challenge to our present-day theories and fixations about the function of words when given poetic intent.

Gilbert White, the naturalist curate of the Hampshire village of Selbourne, in charge of the spiritual welfare of a tiny community at that time enslaved under the squirarchal system, did not allow that way of life to stain the purity of his prose. He could observe that:

Sitting in the entrance of their caverns, field-crickets chirp all night as well as day from the middle of the month of May to the middle of July; and in hot weather, when they are most vigorous, they make the hills echo, and in the stiller hours of darkness may be heard to a considerable distance. In the beginning of the season their notes are more faint and inward; but become louder as the summer advances, and so die away again by degrees.

In both those quotations I detect the magic which hovers over the syllables, like bees and moths, sipping the honey from them and storing it for perpetual nourishment. We can taste it now.

This is no literary device or trick. It is not mere ornament. John Ruskin isolates its distinctive quality in his book *The Seven Lamps of Architecture*. The quotation is from a chapter called *The Lamp of Truth*, an apt sub-title. He is writing about ornament, and

the sense of human labour and care spent upon it. How great this latter influence we may perhaps judge, by considering that there is not a cluster of weeds growing in any cranny of ruin which has not a beauty in all respects *nearly* equal, and in some, immeasurably superior, to that of the most elaborate sculptors of its stones: and that all our interest in the carved work, our sense of its richness, though it is tenfold less rich than the knots of grass beside it; of its delicacy, though it is a thousandfold less delicate; of its admirableness, though a millionfold less admirable; results from our consciousness of its being the work of poor, clumsy, toilsome man. Its true delightfulness depends on our discovering in it the record of thoughts, and intents, and trials, and heart-breakings—of recoveries and joyfulnesses of success: all this *can* be traced by a practised eye; but, granting even obscure, it is presumed or understood; and in that is the worth of the thing, just as much as the worth of anything else we call precious.

That piece of rotund, exfoliating prose, so characteristic of Ruskin's unstable genius, links up the two elements which I am trying to present throughout this essay, the craft and the accretion, the conscious, dutiful, and patient workmanship, and the unexpected, organic addition to its intended result. It is the two in one which presents the art of word-usage, whatever convention, or fashion, or culture may enclose it. It may be ignored by fashions, but it survives them, because it is too elusive to be captured and dissected.

My own autumnal mood, after the lifelong pursuit of this quality within the words, is contained in a passage from Isaac Walton's *The Compleat Angler.* His casting for trout is a parable of my purpose in this essay. It is a parable, and it is also an example, especially in the poem by George Herbert, which he quotes:

> And now, Scholar, my direction for Flie-fishing is ended with this showre, for it has done raining, and now look about you, and see how pleasantly that Meadow looks; nay, and the Earth smells as sweetly too. Come, let me tell you what holy Mr. Herbert sayes of such days and flowers as these, and then we will thank God that we enjoy them, and walk to the River and sit down quietly, and try to catch the other brace of Trout.

> Sweet day, so cool, so calm, so bright,
> The bridal of the earth and skie,
> Sweet dews shall weep they fall to night,
>   for thou must die.

> Sweet Rose, whose hew, angry and brave,
> Bids the rash gazer wipe his eye,
> Thy root is ever in its grave,
>   and thou must die.

> Sweet Spring, full of sweet dayes and roses,
> A box where sweets compacted lye;
> My Music shewes you have your closes,
>   and all must die.

Only a sweet and virtuous soul,
Like seasoned Timber never gives,
But when the whole world turns to cole,
    then chiefly lives.

The magic in that seventeenth-century prose and verse may be inaudible to latterday readers habituated to the strident tones of much modern word-usage, in the Press, in fiction and verse, where so frequently the writer is concerned to present the permissive by being excessive. But the magic is there. Even the caprice of capital letters, perhaps an assumed naivety, perhaps merely customary to the period, adds some drops of dew: but it is spiritual dew, alighting on the words as invisibly as those drops which refresh the wonders of nature:

when out of night earth rolls her dewy sides.

We write and talk mostly in darkness, or at best in twilight, even when youthful and most assured, most bright-eyed. The persuasion of beauty and the authority of truth are imparted to our words by some power outside our conscious intelligence.

Who was it said 'I love you',
And dared to call it truth?
It might be any creature
In the half-light of youth,
When birth's deceptive starlight
Still lures while it deludes,
Before the sky is emptied
By the voracious sun
Whose total light brings blindness
To all save only one:
And who that is, love dare not
Proclaim till life be done.

9

So this effort, in old age, after an active professional life in the use of words, turns out to be a failure to unveil the mystery of language, this gift common, but unique, to the human race. Mankind, in his intercourse, his perpetual activity, uses it. If man were a machine, we could call language the lubricant on which he functions. But we know him to be both more and less than a machine, and language does not always make for smooth running. It can be corrosive. It can poison society and individuals as well as persuade them. It can be prostituted to our passions, so that in times of crises it becomes hardly more than the howling of wolves, and in the mouths of bored or ignorant people, nothing but a grunt. We elide and mutilate our syllables in everyday conversation. In our newspapers and books, we follow the popular modes, which are never interested in excellence, never 'aristocratic', in the true meaning of that word which is execrated today because of its mis-application in the past.

But parallel with this use of language as a utility in everyday life, there has always been this overtone, something that can be heard as an influence from we know not where. But we recognise it. We feel it touching us like sunshine, like rain, like moonlight, and it gives value to life again.

That is why it survives as the vehicle of our ever-increasing purposes, our ever more subtle and complex activities. In spite of it being a common medium, rubbed and worn by abusive and extravagant usage, we find it perpetually clean and malleable as an art-form. In the hands of a skilled orator or writer, or a person with innocent intent, our language can still surprise us, charm us, inspire us, though today it is the articulation of a culture sunk in sophistication and decadence.

This quality, seemingly indestructible, which I have called the overtone of language, as though this human faculty were bell-music, is something which every writer, at his best, seeks after and restores to the words he chooses, whatever his purpose may be. The choice is not always conscious. How it functions remains outside the determinations of will, of intellect, of cultural background and sensibility.

It may be a combination of all these factors, as a child epitomises its ancestry, but with something new added. That something new is a personal supplement to the general body of our mother-tongue. We never weary of looking for it.

I saw an example of this alertness in a tiny lyric, appropriately entitled 'Search' in a collection of poems by a contemporary, Jack Bevan. Here is what he says,

> When she is with me, I never see her,
> Parted, I found her everywhere,
> Each stone a milestone, every tree her
> Calendar, Now all is bare.
> Now she is near I never see her,
> When I can see her, she isn't there.

That little poem is also an example of the depth beyond depth of reference which words can explore when used with wisdom and simplicity. Their application becomes universal. The lover can see the truth in that poem, when he or she discovers the fact that it is often easier to recall the features of mere acquaintances, than those of husband, wife or children, in absence, or after death.

I have used it, equally validly, as an allegory, representing this elusive conjuration latent in every word, every syllable, no matter how rubbed and defaced by common use

> From early days,
> Beginning not long after that first time
> In which, a Babe, by intercourse of touch
> I held mute dialogues with my Mother's heart,
> I have endeavoured to display the means
> Whereby this infant sensibility,
> Great birthright of our being, was in me
> Augmented and sustained.

That passage from Wordsworth's autobiographical poem 'The Prelude' can have the same reference as *I* have given to Mr. Bevan's poem. 'The infant sensibility' is the tap-root of all art, and sustains it, whatever its medium may be, and however complex and sophisticated its later growth.

We build our careers upon those first intimations, obeying as well as directing that 'infant sensibility'. Everybody acknowledges the dual authority within himself. The artist, because his vocation makes him more emphatically a self-searcher, learns to balance the two powers, so that they interact harmoniously, the sub-conscious, intuitive 'infant sensibility' remaining innocent, naive, through adult life and experience, but resourceful and able to make the conscious self 'surprised by joy' even when experience has become a burden, heavy with sorrows; to balance that with the effort to understand, to control our environment, and to make of it, through the faith lodged in those intentions, something durable, maybe even beautiful.

This is the function of every human life, indeed of all organic life. There is no new discovery in this acknowledgment, but the rhythm of it, the interplay of inspiration and intellectual control, needs constantly to be observed, and if possible, defined, if only to prevent us from falling into scepticism, and to take the material of life for granted, forgetting that it is miraculous.

That basic miracle, too, is latent in the words we use, 'though when I see her, she isn't there'. The purpose of a writer is to use words, believing that she *is* there, a Presence that first became apparent in that 'infant sensibility'. That Presence is indefinable, but it may be symbolised by the waters of a river: always there, never there; always the same, always different.

It is thus, with our flow of words. The writer's concern is to keep that flow unimpeded by ideologies, unpolluted by the clogging degradations of an over-sophisticated culture, a weary society.

Wordsworth's valedictory sonnet to the River Duddon

expresses my feeling towards the words which I have tried to
catch in a sieve.

I thought of Thee, my partner and my guide,
As being passed away—Vain sympathies!
For, backward Duddon! as I cast my eyes,
I see what was, and is, and will abide;
Still glides the Stream, and shall for ever glide;
The Form remains, the Function never dies;
While we, the brave, the mighty, and the wise,
We Men, who in our morn of youth defied
The elements, must vanish;—be it so!
Enough, if something from our hands have power
To live, and act, and serve the future hour;
And if, as toward the silent tomb we go,
Through love, through hope, and faith's transcendent dower,
We feel that we are greater than we know.